**JUMP**
and
**find**
Joy

## ALSO BY HODA KOTB

*Hope Is a Rainbow*

*This Just Speaks to Me: Words to Live By Every Day*

*I Really Needed This Today: Words to Live By*

*You Are My Happy*

*I've Loved You Since Forever*

*Where We Belong:*
*Journeys That Show Us the Way*

*Ten Years Later: Six People*
*Who Faced Adversity and Transformed Their Lives*

*Hoda: How I Survived War Zones,*
*Bad Hair, Cancer, and Kathie Lee*

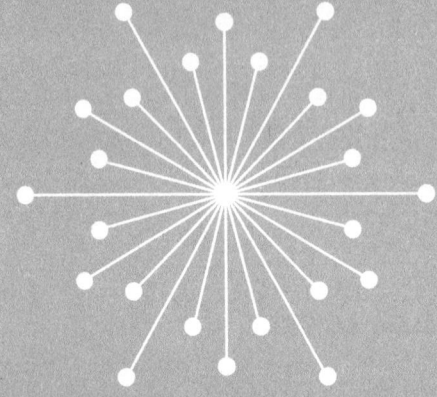

# HODA KOTB

## WITH JANE LORENZINI.

# JUMP
## and
## find
# Joy

—

## Embracing Change
## in Every Season
## of Life

G. P. PUTNAM'S SONS

New York

## PUTNAM
— EST. 1838 —

G. P. PUTNAM'S SONS
*Publishers Since 1838*
An imprint of Penguin Random House LLC
1745 Broadway, New York, NY 10019
penguinrandomhouse.com

BOOK DESIGN BY KATY RIEGEL

LIBRARY OF CONGRESS CATALOGING-IN-PUBLICATION DATA
has been requested.

Hardcover ISBN: 9798217043880
Ebook ISBN: 9798217043897
Target edition ISBN: 9798217180318

Printed in the United States of America
2nd Printing

The authorized representative in the EU for product safety and compliance
is Penguin Random House Ireland, Morrison Chambers, 32 Nassau Street,
Dublin D02 YH68, Ireland, https://eu-contact.penguin.ie.

*This book is dedicated to you, my darling.*

*Curious, hopeful, determined you.*

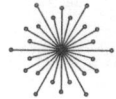

# Contents

# CONTENTS

# CONTENTS

# CONTENTS

# Introduction:
# Right on Time

READY, SET . . . JUMP!

I can still picture my younger self holding hands with my sister, Hala, counting down, then jumping feet first into the town pool, screaming our heads off. We did it! Now I watch my two daughters do the same thing at the beach, launching themselves off the pier into the sparkling water below. Boy, taking a big leap when you're a kid is easy, isn't it? And so much fun! But later, as we get older and tethered to the world we've built, jumping can be harder . . . and scary. So, we stay put. No butterflies. No wind in our hair. No big splash. Bummer.

Chances are there've been times in your life when you've wondered if things could be different . . . better. You gaze down at that imaginary water and think, *Should I just go for it? Will I drown? Am I crazy?* Those big—and even small—jumps can feel risky. After all, if making any sort of leap was simple, most of us would have done it by now. Who doesn't want to exist on a richer, deeper, more joyous level? But redrawing the blueprints of our life tends to be a "someday" project, rolled up and set aside as we focus instead on making it through the week. If only there were a pause button so we could do some deep thinking. Or even better, an extended time-out for transformation! But the truth is, we stay relentlessly busy juggling family, work, friendships, and on and on.

Most of us only daydream about a bolder, brighter existence. It's easy to forget—or deny—that *we* are the architects of our destiny. As leadership coach Shailja Sharma writes, "No matter the difficulties you may be facing, remember you are still a conscious creator of your life."

I've always been interested in—and inspired by—conscious creators. People who've managed to pivot in ways that result in a meaningful rebirth of their heart and soul. *How did they do it? What powered their courage?* Fortunately, over the course of my decades-long career as a journalist, I've spoken with some of these incredible people—artists, entertainers, innovators, spiritual leaders, and deep thinkers; those who've faced moments of intense doubt and responded with great courage. What I've learned from each of them is this: Change is not only exciting— it's essential. And the right changes happen right on time.

I had just turned sixty when change tracked me down and stamped a big red RIGHT TIME on my heart. *Bam!* The message was loud and clear, and you know what? I was ready for it. It *was* the right time.

Truth was, I'd been allowing myself for a few years to wonder what my world would feel like if—after twenty-six years— I parted ways with the Peacock. If, for the first time, I didn't renegotiate my contract. Would I desperately miss NBC and my beloved coworkers? If I left journalism, how would I continue to connect with people and stay current? Anyone in my position, who's enjoyed a meaningful professional life, wrestles with the idea of moving on from the routine and rewards that years of hard work have brought them. And I *did* struggle for a while, pondering my exit but always postponing it. After all, my various positions at NBC were so different—*Dateline*; cohosting *Today* with Kathie Lee, then Savannah, and then Jenna. My work life never felt stale. There was no *yawn*. Time just kept flying by, and I felt fortunate to have the very best jobs in television.

But, after I adopted my kids, my perspective on work—and everything—changed. How could it not? Like anyone who experiences parenthood for the first time, I fell head over heels in love with my children. My heart totally Grinched out—it grew three sizes after I met those babies. Instantly, my priorities forked in a profound way. Work was still important, but now I had two little cuties filling up the Mommy Bucket I'd dreamed of for so long. Family had always been important to me, but now I was raising my own . . . and I wanted to do it well. And on my terms.

It was in 2024 that my decision to move on from NBC became crystal clear. The decade of my sixties had arrived, and I'd been thinking and journaling about what that would look like for me: a clean slate waiting for plans. Would I feel more financially secure if I signed another contract extension? Yes. Did I love my coworkers, our viewers, and all the extraordinary assignments I was given? Yes. But what so powerfully countered every *yes* were the amazing sights and sounds unfolding before me in my fresh start outside of the Big Apple. Suddenly, I knew there was more, something different. Special. *New.*

In August 2024, after my girls and I moved out of bustling Manhattan to the leafy suburbs, I watched them climb trees and play nonstop on their backyard swing set. Birds were singing, and the air smelled like cut grass (and whatever my neighbors were barbecuing). Freshly baked pies appeared on my doorstep. Heavenly! Those small-town vibes were activating my imagination about what my next step could look like. I pictured myself walking the kids to school each morning and volunteering at their recitals and sporting events. Instead of needing octopus arms to manage a million things, I could just be Mom, present and focused, with my *two* arms wrapped around my daughters. When you wait so long to be a parent like I did, it's hard to justify missing even the most basic stuff. Every little moment feels important.

When that RIGHT TIME rubber-stamp moment happened, Haley was seven and Hope was five. Work in 2024 had been particularly busy, including a trip to Bermuda with Jenna, plus a glorious two-week stint in Paris covering the Olympics. Just one day after I returned home from the games, I was grateful to wake up to a meaningful milestone—my sixtieth birthday. That weekend, the girls' dad, Joel, joined my family and a few close friends to grill out and devour cake. The best! On that Monday, NBC hosted a supersized celebration and spoiled me rotten. The birthday bash they threw for me out on the plaza was absolutely mind-blowing. The amount of planning that went into that party was extraordinary, and, as usual, it was perfectly executed by my work family. Even the weather was spot-on! Surprise after surprise kept unfolding before me, and a heady mix of emotions joined in the fun—joy, gratitude, excitement, awe. I couldn't believe that folks had driven or flown to New York to share in the festivities, many of whom I'd never met. Even my college mascot showed up, for goodness' sake. Every minute was surreal.

That day, I looked out at a sea of hand-drawn signs and the shining faces of the people waving them. My favorite bands rocked the crowd and dear friends popped up out of nowhere. Throughout, a string of videos playing on the wayback machine captured the countless people and places that I'd grown to love during so many years working at NBC. And my daughters were there for it all. While I was bawling absolute tears of joy, my heart was bursting, too. In an out-of-body sort of way, I experienced a very deep rush of elation and realization: this magical day was without a doubt the top of the professional wave for me, and I was riding the crest right there on the plaza. It was the bomb! I knew right then and there, *It can't get any better for me than it is at this very moment.* And it felt awesome. I knew this was indeed *the right time* to move on.

The following month, I shared my decision with my bosses, and then with our viewers. The outpouring of love and support was truly humbling. People wished me the best and seemed to understand why I was leaving. I had kids who needed me more than ever, my mom was getting older, and frankly, it would be nice not to see the number 3 when I set my alarm each night. In my new life, I'd have total control over how to slice up my time pie, and the idea of finally having that flexibility felt incredible. Still, like so many of you, I'm a worker at heart. Rolling up my sleeves and contributing in some way has always been and will always be baked into my life plan. So, now what?

Where exactly was I headed professionally? Interestingly, it was an experience I'd had five years earlier that became the launching pad for my new and exciting work adventure.

During my early fifties, I just assumed I was wired to be high-strung and half nuts—a real control freak. Physical exercise helped calm me, but there were only so many miles I could run or ride a week! I resigned myself to the fact that it was just in my nature to be stressed and on edge. But, one day, everything changed. Hearing me lament (again) my always-on state of mind, Jenna suggested I try something she loved that didn't involve any cardio at all: a breathwork class. *Huh? I know how to breathe, Jenna.* But I went, and to my complete surprise, a simple technique changed everything for me. In the class, I learned how to inhale through my mouth, pause, then exhale as if I were blowing on a spoonful of hot soup. It was easy and somehow effective! I continued to practice, and in no time at all, this new partnership with my lungs rewired me to be more relaxed and focused. To boot, this mindful breathing stuff was free and doable anywhere.

I began to wonder what else was out there that could simply—and cheaply—enhance daily life for all of us. I read a ton of books and listened to countless podcasts about the power of pursuing wellness in new and different ways. The research was thrilling and inspiring and my new adventure began to reveal itself. By age sixty, I was a breathing, meditating believer! What eventually took shape was a multipronged mission to expose people to easy and affordable ways to launch a wellness journey tailored to *their* individual personalities and needs. I decided to call my venture Joy 101.

This pivot into everyday wellness has been transformative for me, and it only began because I took a chance and tried something new. Honestly, I guess I've always been willing to experience anything and everything because that approach to life has served me well. The most meaningful growth for me has been rooted in having an open mind and heart. And the leaps of faith I've taken have always paid off in such beautiful ways.

But it's important to point out that I've certainly relied on others to teach and inspire me as I've considered making a change. Throughout my life, I've always been on the lookout for the people who've jumped before me, pioneers who blazed a trail that was beckoning me. I truly believe that role models serve as an effective shock absorber when our soul is yearning for something. Especially when that "something" alarms and upsets the brain. *Nope. We're not doing that.* But when we see someone who's pulled off what we're considering, our brain dials back its concern. The leap seems less risky. *Oh, okay. That's what it looks like on the other side.*

For example, every time I relocated for work, I remembered how successfully my parents moved our family around the world and within the United States. Then, when I launched my healing journey following breast cancer, I looked for vibrant survivors who were running marathons or engaging in whatever they loved. My dream of adopting kids became clearer when I saw that actress Sandra Bullock had done it later in life. We all want a peek at the other side, right? I remember Andy Cohen called me after I adopted my girls and asked me what it was like parenting at our age. I guess I was one of *his* shock absorbers. *Okay, she landed smoothly.*

So, as I was mentally preparing for my big jump toward wellness, I kept booking guests on my podcast who'd taken a risk or a big swing at something well outside their comfort zone. I was fascinated and fueled by their courage. These conversations were pumping me up! I started thinking about how to share their stories—and my own—with anyone else who was considering transformation. So many people I knew were. Ultimately, the answer was to capture these inspiring messages I was hearing and harness this powerful momentum I was feeling in a book. *This* book. And curiously, as I began to write these pages, the process revealed that I've *always* had a sometimes scary but always satisfying relationship with change. Story after story confirmed that I've had a pretty darn good track record with leaping and landing. That my gut has always been a very reliable partner. Today, I feel more strongly than ever that our lives *can* be better when we open ourselves to change. That it's never too late to thrive. In the words of writer Joseph Campbell, "We must be willing to let go of the life we planned so as to have the life that is waiting for us."

So, what's waiting for you? Are you feeling curious or cautious or completely confused about how to transform your life in a big or small way? Would you like some company? Well, cozy up and carry on. In the pages ahead, you'll share in the meaningful conversations I've had with a broad range of people who've both resisted and embraced change. I'll also reflect on my own experience with considering whether to stay put or launch forward. You'll meet the people whose inspiring jumps— *jumpstarts*—have motivated me to make a personal or professional move. Ideally, many of these stories will serve as a source of guidance or motivation for you, too. A first step. I truly believe that it's never too late to let go of what you know isn't working and go for what you want. As author Deborah Day writes, "Recognizing that you are not where you want to be is a starting point to begin changing your life."

So, what do you say? Let's start. Take my hand.

Ready, set . . . jump!

# Part 1

## A Jumping-Off Point

The expression "Look before you leap!" sounds old-timey, but to me, the meaning of it never goes out of style. It's good advice! Before you jump into something new, you need to make a plan, check out what's ahead, and be sure you're heading in the right direction. Ask yourself: *Am I where I want to be, doing what I want to be doing, with the people I want to be doing it with?* The answer to all those questions may be yes, but I think it's valuable to be curious, to explore if there could be something more. Maybe you're feeling like a little African violet, outgrowing your pot, ready to put down roots somewhere new. Or maybe you consider your life to be fine, just fine . . . when it could be fantastic.

I think we're wired to follow the if-it-ain't-broke-don't-fix-it strategy. But that can keep us stuck in a so-so situation for far too long. Something I've learned along the way is, maybe we don't need to wait for something to break to make a meaningful leap. Maybe we can jump *toward* something instead of just staying put. As one of my favorite expressions suggests, "It is never too late to be what you might have been."

I know it can be draining to contemplate life, as opposed to just living it. But taking time to fully and truthfully examine where you are can prevent you from sliding into predictable patterns or putting up with what you know you shouldn't. Taking stock of your circumstances can also confirm what *is* working for you, and it reminds you of what you love and are grateful for. So, try to be honest with yourself. Your journey is entirely your own and unique, like you. Only you know what makes you happy and feel fulfilled.

So, yes—before you jump, look around at your life. But then take a good look inside yourself, too. Well, what do you know . . . this is getting exciting!

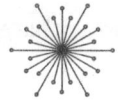

## MOVED TO MAKE A CHANGE

Change is something I was exposed to very early on in my life, and I never thought of it as scary. When I was a kid, my family moved from one country to another. We bounced around from city to city, following my dad's work. Relocating so frequently left a major impression on me as an adult, and in the best way possible. It showed me that traveling and experiencing the world was within my reach. All I needed was a plane ticket or a full tank of gas and I could be somewhere new!

All that uprooting wasn't always easy, but I found that over time transitions throughout life are certainly doable. Now you can send me anywhere and it won't take me too long to find my footing. I think that's because I see moving as an opportunity, not an obstacle. And I have my parents to thank for that.

My mom and dad, Sameha and Abdel Kotb, were movers and shakers right from the start. From meeting at a law firm in Cairo after college, to falling in love at my dad's boat race along the Nile River, to getting married among the pyramids, they've always been people of action. The fact that they moved to the United States just one week after getting married to pursue a new life together proves the point! But just because they were doers doesn't mean that they weren't also thinkers. They thought long and hard about the decisions they made as a couple, and later the choices they made for us as a family. However, when I was a kid, some of their decisions seemed suspect. When your parents tell you in fourth grade that you're going back to Egypt and then to Nigeria for six months because Dad has a job opportunity, the first thing that comes to mind isn't, "Awesome!" It's more like, "OMG, this is so unfair!"

But now that I'm an adult and a parent, I know how much planning went into their transitions. Before that first big move they made from Egypt to America, they looked before they leaped. It would have been so easy for my mom and dad to just stay in Cairo because things were going well for them there. They worked at the same law firm, were surrounded by family who loved them, and were starting their life together as newlyweds. It would have made sense to look around and say, "Yup, we're good!" But instead, they imagined an even better life. While grateful for all they had in Egypt, my parents decided they wanted something more—something that required a bold plan. Like so many immigrants before them, that meant a move to America.

My dad would get his PhD at the University of Oklahoma, where a full scholarship awaited him. They would leave the busy metropolis of Cairo for Norman, Oklahoma, but they would never leave behind the strong work ethic they'd learned from family. My mother's father was a supreme court judge. Her mother was a doctor and her aunt was the first female lawyer in Egypt. My mom witnessed firsthand that it was possible to carve her own path—anywhere—if she was persistent. Unfortunately, her law degree wasn't valid in the United States, so she decided to tap into her love of books and pursue a master's degree in library science. A fresh start in America meant that both my parents would be students once again. But, as newly-weds, they knew that furthering their education before starting a family here was the right thing to do.

I'm so glad my parents looked before they leaped, giving them the confidence they needed to make important decisions. That's what I've always done, too, whether it's a move across the country for work or a move to the suburbs for a new home with my girls. My approach is to be cautious but courageous.

Don't you think we can sometimes talk ourselves into set-tling? *This is it. And that's fine.* We tell ourselves that as long as things aren't terrible, we should be satisfied; that wanting more is greedy. But I think it's always valuable to wonder. *Am I living my best life? Does it make sense for who I am now?* To me, won-dering is not rooted in greed; it's rooted in growth.

That mindset of wonder makes me think about a point in my dad's life when he worked as a professor at West Virginia University. We'd been living a happy life in West Virginia—or so I thought—when my parents decided that we were going to move to a suburb outside of Washington, DC. We kids didn't understand didn't understand and were so upset, but my par-ents explained that the decision had been made: we were going to live and work in Alexandria, Virginia, several hours and a world away from the West Virginia town we'd called home for what seemed like forever. Many years would pass before my siblings and I figured out why.

After my dad died suddenly at age fifty-two, my brother, Adel, was cleaning out his work desk and found a letter that my father had written to his bosses. At the time, he was the chair-man of the Department of Petroleum Engineering at WVU.

The letter addressed his salary, which was the lowest on staff, even though he had his doctorate and some of the other professors didn't. He had apparently looked around and realized that he deserved a promotion. No one was offering it to him, so he was going to ask for one. In the letter, he outlined his credentials and kindly requested to be brought up to scale with his colleagues.

But his request was denied. His superiors wrote back, saying essentially that he was earning all he was ever going to make. There would be no raise. There would be no promotion. There was no room for growth. So, my dad decided that if he couldn't go upward, he'd go onward, and we moved to Virginia.

And here's the amazing part. My father never shared with us that his bosses said he was earning all that they felt he deserved. He never told us that sometimes the world is unfair and *oh well*. He could have stayed at WVU and taught us that we're better off just accepting the status quo. But he didn't.

If he had, I might have felt differently about my own rejections when I was starting my job hunt years later. I may have put limits on myself and given in to other people's ideas of how far I could go. But I didn't. I had no bitterness or defeatism weighing me down when the time came for me to pursue my career. When things didn't work out, I knew that I had to keep moving forward and try something else. My mantra: *onward*—just like my dad.

I adored him, and like many kids who idolize their fathers, I thought there was nothing he couldn't do. I used to dream that my dad was the president of the United States! (Even though I knew he wasn't eligible, having been born outside the country.) But as I was to find out, he did indeed have presidential ambitions, even if they weren't political. Never one to shy away from change, when he was fifty years old, my dad made another big decision: he left his stable government job at the US Department of Energy to start his own company. I know it wasn't an easy decision; the government benefits and professional stability were appealing. Who would want to leave all that? But once again, Dad looked around and knew that there were more challenges he wanted to tackle. So, he started IPCS, International Petroleum Consulting Services. Now he was his own boss. Shortly after he started his company, I noticed his business card. The title on it: PRESIDENT. I knew he could do it! My dad was always at the top of his game. He had a dream, and he was bold enough to embrace change yet again and to make it happen. (I gotta say, that good man has always been my hero.)

To be clear, it's important to point out that in the middle of all these changes my family made—and that I've made—there was a lot of adjusting. Nobody sticks the landing right away, and that's okay. It takes time to find your footing with any new challenge or in any new place. But the idea is to feel good about your decision to jump because you looked first. Confidence is the key to trusting that the change you're about to make is the right one—at least for right now.

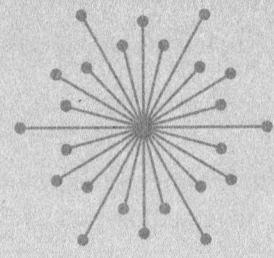

**"Go confidently in the direction of your dreams!**

**Live the life you've imagined."**

—Henry David Thoreau

# Jumpstart

## ANNE LAMOTT

I love spending time with bestselling author Anne Lamott, who lives her life like an open book. She's honest and vulnerable and there's just something about her writing that always fills me up. So often she redefines the messy piles in our lives as little bundles of kindling that can fuel personal growth and spark gratitude. She's beyond wise, and I'm always excited to hear her perspective on anything and everything, including the topic of love.

When I interviewed Anne in 2021, I asked her how she approached dating during her decades of being single.

"It was always secretly a dream to find someone who's your soulmate and your partner," she said. "So, when it happened, I thought, *Okay, what's the catch?*"

Turns out, Anne had finally found the right approach to selecting a mate for life. She said in the past, she'd chosen men who could never quite capture her whole heart. But, through years of learning from failed relationships, she set a new standard for choosing a husband.

"I wanted to find a man who, if he was a woman, I would have wanted to be best friends with," she explained. "And that is, in fact, what I found in Neal."

Anne met Neal Allen on Match.com, a popular dating site. Two years after their first date, Neal proposed while they were watching the US Open on television. When they married in 2019, she became a newlywed for the first time at the age of sixty-five! While Anne jokes that she got married three days after receiving Medicare, you know what I say? Your leap to forever love was right on time, Annie!

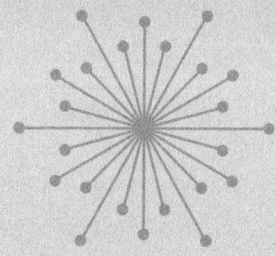

**"Love is a friendship set to music."**

—Joseph Campbell

# Jumpstart

## BETTE MIDLER

Big leaps deserve lots of focus, but even small hops require some reflection. After all, small daily decisions can add up and affect our quality of life. Like adding five minutes to your morning walk or swapping mustard for mayo—mini changes that might seem insignificant but that can have a big impact on our lives.

In 2024, during an interview with legendary actress and singer Bette Midler, one of her responses reminded me of that sort of "micro" managing. The two of us were laughing about the hilarious character she plays in the movie *The Fabulous Four*, a bride-to-be who's obsessed with TikTok. When I asked Bette how she personally felt about using the platform, she said, "I tried. I gave it a few hours of my life and thought, *This is too dangerous.* I looked up and asked, 'What time is it?' Someone said it was four, and I was like, 'But how can it be?!'"

We've all been there, Bette. Ticktock! It only took one look for the Divine Miss M to know that this particular time suck was not for her. So she jumped away from that app—for good. (Although I have to say, if Bette Midler did have a TikTok channel, I'd watch it!)

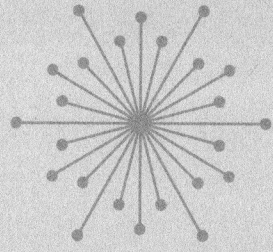

**"Don't follow a trend. Follow your heart."**

—*Krist Novoselic*

## YOUR FIRST LEAP WON'T BE YOUR LAST

I've always known that I wanted to pursue a career that connected me with people. When I was very young, I thought that was teaching. I'd imagine myself in a classroom filled with kids leading the charge! (Only later in life did I realize that wanting to be a teacher was actually me wanting to be a mom.) When it came time to determine a direction in college, I was drawn to courses in writing and reporting. As it turned out, journalism was my jam. To this day, it gets my blood pumping and my brain firing. It allows me to connect, share, and learn all at the same time.

But, many years before I finally found my way to 30 Rockefeller Center, I burned a lot of gas and time trying to find someone, *anyone*, who would give me my first job in broadcast journalism.

When I graduated from college, I thought my dive into the "real world" would be quick and easy, so I only lined up one job interview. I was golden! After all, everyone I knew had gotten a job offer, so I'd get one, too, right? And definitely in a top-tier television market. All I needed to do was show up with my mad skills and wow them. Well . . .

Let's back it up. The year is 1987. I've graduated from college and returned home after a year living with my aunt and uncle in Egypt, where I did anything and everything I could at the

CBS news station for a year. Those brief highlights of my very first journalistic efforts are proudly featured on my résumé, a giant VHS tape. (Remember those big, clunky things?)

The day of my first—and only—interview in Richmond, Virginia, has arrived. I get my hair blown out, put on my new green suit, borrow my mom's car, and hit the road. Let's go! My interview is an hour and a half away, but I fully expect to be back by dinnertime with a job offer and a reason to celebrate. Shoulders back, head held high, I march into that newsroom and meet with the news director, confident that he'll soon be my boss! I hand him my tape and wait for him to be impressed.

But no sooner than he pops it in, he pops it back out, missing at least twenty-five of the twenty-seven minutes of my very best on-air work. Apparently, that's all the time he needed to determine that he's *not* my new boss. According to him, I'm way too green . . . and he doesn't mean my brand-new suit. He explains that Richmond is a top one hundred market, and apparently, I'm not ready to work anywhere near the top. I'm shocked! Stunned! My first dive into broadcasting is more like a belly flop.

When I manage to ask what I can do to improve, he says, "Get more experience." So, with my tape in my hand and a lump in my throat, I start to leave. But he stops me. He has a friend in Roanoke, Virginia, three hours away, who's looking for someone. If I can get there before his pal leaves for a trip the next day, he'll arrange an interview. Do I think I can make it?

*Can I?* Well, I still have gas in the tank, and my pretty green suit and blowout are no worse for wear. I call my mom, who cheers me on. *You can do it!* And I get back out on the road.

Roanoke, Virginia. Okay. It's no Richmond, but I can make

it work. Surely, the second time is the charm. But, when I arrive, once again . . . ouch! The news director tells me right away that I'm years from a job in Roanoke. Years! *Ugh.* But before I tuck tail and leave, thankfully, another door creaks open. A guy on staff in Roanoke says he has a buddy who happens to be hiring in Memphis. The only problem is that *he's* going to a conference the next day (why were these news directors always jetting off somewhere?), but if I can catch the guy before he leaves, I might just get hired in the Memphis market. So, Tennessee, here I come!

Now, it's a twelve-hour drive from Roanoke to Memphis— in the opposite direction of my home—and it's getting late. I call my mom, tell her I need her car a little longer, and start driving. When I finally arrive, looking quite road-weary (my suit and hair tapped out a few miles back), I wash up in a gas station and make my way to the interview. The news director tells me he has ten minutes before he leaves to catch a plane. Ten minutes—plenty of time! But, after one minute of watching that darn VHS tape—you guessed it—I'm not ready for Memphis. Holy moly.

Reality is starting to sink in. I guess it's time to adjust my expectations. I'm still going to jump, but just not as high or as far or as fast as I anticipated. Not even close. After ten days of driving and multiple rejections—in Birmingham and Dothan, Alabama, plus a few markets in the Florida panhandle—I'm experiencing all the feels. Rejected. Defeated. Frustrated. Finally, I decide to make the long journey back home. It's time. As I'm driving along and feeling lost in the world, I actually *get* lost. I have no idea where I am. *Groan.* I'm exhausted and the universe is trying to tell me (twenty-seven times) that my broadcasting dream is a bust and that I should go into public relations.

But suddenly, out of the blue, while driving through Mississippi, I see a sign. A billboard that reads: *Our Eye Is on You, Greenville, WXVT.* Hmm. Is this massive sign also some sort of cosmic sign? I feel a jolt of adrenaline and think, *I've come this far. Why don't I just go to Greenville, Mississippi, and get rejected one more time—but quickly, because my mom needs the car.* So, I find my way to WXVT and drag myself into the newsroom, tired and full of doubt. Right away, a cheerful man approaches me and puts out his hand for a shake.

"Hi, I'm Stan Sandroni! I was the sports director yesterday, but they've promoted me to news director. What's your name?"

"Hoda."

"Hi, Hilda! Let's see what you've got on this tape."

*Sure, Stan,* I think. *Why not. You can be the guy who makes it an even twenty-eight rejections.* I hand him the tape and wait for him to eject it and reject me. But then, at the place where everyone else stopped watching, Stan stuns me. He *keeps* watching. He watches the whole damn thing! When it ends, he turns to me and says, "Hilda—"

"Hoda . . ."

"I like what I see!"

"You do?" I ask, and explode into tears.

Twenty-seven rejections for a twenty-seven-minute tape! It must've been some kind of record. But all it took was one person to watch the entire video, see some potential, and give me that one *yes* I'd been driving around the whole of the southeastern US hoping to hear.

I listen as Stan lays out our plan.

"Okay, so first, you're going to meet Joe; he's the general manager, and if he says yes, then you're going to be the Greenwood, Mississippi, bureau chief. Not Greenville, that's the big city. Greenwood."

*Greenwood.*

"You're going to the smaller place."

*Smaller than Greenville?*

"And you're going to be in charge."

*Well, okay! Hallelujah!*

Sure, the city and salary are smaller than I imagined—I probably made more money working at Ponderosa—but I don't care. I'm the new bureau chief! And the photographer, and hair and makeup, and wardrobe, and it's all perfect.

I'll never forget that crazy road trip or Stan Sandroni. That wonderful guy took a long, close look at my work and then took a leap of faith—a big one—for me.

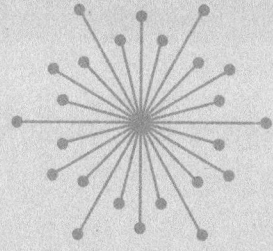

"The most important key to achieving great

success is to decide upon your goal and

launch, get started, take action, move."

—Brian Tracy

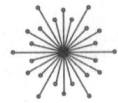

## THINK BEFORE YOU JUMP

So many emotions bubble up when you start anything new. Life feels exciting and inside you're yelling, *Game on!* But being a rookie can also make it seem like you have zero power and that you're just lucky to have been chosen. Pumped and hungry, you do whatever it takes to move up the ladder.

That was me after a year of working at Newscenter 15 in Greenville, Mississippi. One day I got a call to interview with the news director at Active 8 in Moline, Illinois. *Yes!* WQAD was in a bigger market, and this was my chance to advance my career. I was so excited! Well, wouldn't you know it, a southern freeze set in and threw a frigid wrench into my travel plans. I had to make a flight out of Memphis, which in good conditions is a nearly three-hour drive from Greenville. But I was determined to catch that plane.

I found out quickly, though, that the roads between Mississippi and Tennessee were like ice-skating rinks. I drove about two miles per hour, creeping along with chains on my tires, trying to avoid slipping into a ditch. But the ice was so hard that the chains kept popping off! My repeated attempts to reengage them failed, the loose chains slapping at the ice. It was slow going but I was determined (or should I say *stubborn*). After all, John Riches and my new job were waiting for me!

I'd left for Memphis the evening before my scheduled flight, so after driving all night I finally made it to the Memphis air-port at 7 a.m.—just in time to catch my plane to Illinois. I arrived in Moline and hustled to my interview. It was a crazy thing to do. Any rational person would've rescheduled, and Active 8 would have understood. Looking back, I was very lucky.

And yes, I got the job. But yikes. I would never take a risk like that now. When we're younger or starting out we often think that we have to jump at every opportunity that comes our way. We tell ourselves that if we don't, another chance might not come along. But as we get older, we realize that we don't have to make stupid, reckless jumps. We rarely have "one shot" at something, and putting ourselves in danger or pushing too hard for fear you'll miss out isn't usually worth it. Few of us can sustain a relentless, breakneck pace for long without burning out or making a mistake.

It's like what I learned when I played basketball in high school. As a freshman, I'd spend all my time running around and becoming exhausted. But by my senior year, I knew when to sprint—and when to pause. I was playing smarter. Eventually, you become more measured in how you pace yourself and manage your expectations. (Like, don't mess with Mother Nature.) That's the great thing about getting older—you get wiser, too.

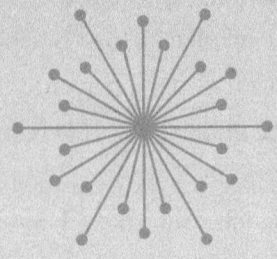

**"Experience is a great teacher."**

—John Legend

# Jumpstart

### CHIP CONLEY

If there's someone who knows all about getting older and wiser—and happier—it's Chip Conley. He's a bestselling author and cofounder of the Modern Elder Academy, touted as the world's first midlife wisdom school. When I spoke to him in 2024, he told me that he's on a mission to reframe midlife, and that everything can be greater *later* when we treat aging as an opportunity, not a crisis.

"One of the things that I learned in my midlife is that my definition of success has changed. I like to call the cultural imprint of success 'successism,'" he explained. "Successism is this thing that says, 'Oh, you gotta keep up with the Joneses,' but what if you don't want to do what the Joneses are doing? What if your definition of success is not having a better BMW than your neighbors? What if your definition of success relates to how it makes you feel about doing things that actually make the world a better place or make you a more interesting person?"

During our conversation, Chip joked that midlife is the "Rodney Dangerfield" of life stages—it don't get no respect. But he considers that a false narrative that needs extensive rebranding. In his book *Learning to Love Midlife: 12 Reasons Why Life Gets Better with Age*, Chip urges us to embrace the opportunity to transform ourselves later in life, armed with the wisdom we've gained over time.

"As we get older, our emotional intelligence gets better," he said. "As we get older, our wisdom grows. We're more compassionate, we have more spiritual curiosity. These are the things that get better with age."

Chip says that living for decades hones what's called our "environmental mastery," an invaluable tool when we want to create change in our lives.

"As we get older, we get better at knowing what habitats we flourish in. Whether that's the community we live in or the career we're in, the friends we have," he said. "We get better at understanding how that habitat will allow us to flourish."

Pretty great, right? No matter what our age, considering a jump is healthy. Just don't forget to look inside, where all the oomph is stored. For those of us in our later years, our vast life experience and deep wisdom are very powerful rocket boosters!

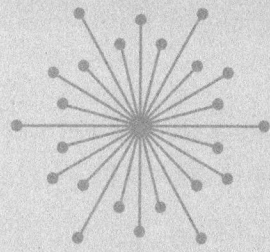

**"Aging is not lost youth but a new stage of opportunity and strength."**

—Betty Friedan

## IT MAY NOT BE BROKEN,
## BUT IT MAY NOT BE WORKING

Wisdom isn't the only thing that comes with getting older; there can be pressure, too. Pressure to *be* certain things or *do* certain things at a particular stage in our lives. Could be at work or in our personal relationships, but that pressure isn't always pushing us in a direction that's right for us.

For many years, I thought of romantic relationships as my sidecar—a nice "extra" thing in my life, but not the main event. After all, as my career started moving faster—Moline to Fort Myers to New Orleans—my job took up most of my time and focus, and that's how I liked it. I was in the driver's seat of my futuremobile, mapping my own course and having a blast doing it. And on the side was this little extra vehicle, a sidecar that might (or often might not) have someone in it. If you've ever ridden in a sidecar, you know that it's fine for a short distance, but it's not really where you want to be for a long journey. There's not a lot of room and it's hard to stretch out and get comfortable. Serious relationships can't be treated like an add-on. Those take time and energy, not to mention space. Sidecar? Not a lot of space.

The fact is that for a long time, I didn't have a lot of space in my life for a serious relationship. And I also didn't think that I really needed one. I was good. I was thrilled with my career and all the great people that I got to work with day in and day out, not to mention all the different cities I got to live in. I enjoyed so many of the spots I spent time in as a young reporter, but when I made it to New Orleans—whew, that really felt like home to me. Oh, how I love that city! To this day, when I fly in, my pulse beats faster as the plane descends and I get closer and closer to soaking up those free-spirited vibes and inhaling my favorite Cajun dishes. Shortly after arriving in New Orleans, I'd fallen hard and given the city—and only the city—my heart. I was happy to go on dates now and then, but I wasn't looking for a love match. Still, somehow, I found myself at a singles' Valentine's Day dance one night.

I remember seeing this guy across the room. He looked like Omar Sharif, which was totally my type at the time. Turns out, we went from dancing to dating, and because he was a busy guy with his own career and I was on the go with mine, for a long time it worked. He and I shared a love for discovering new restaurants and working up a sweat on the tennis court. You'd always find us at whatever festival was rocking New Orleans. We had our ups and downs like everyone else, but for the most part, it was fine.

*Fine.* Do you remember what I said about riding in a sidecar? It's *fine* for a short distance. But you don't build a great romance on fine. You don't get married on fine. Unless, of course, you're not really looking around and taking stock of what's actually in front of you, and you've convinced yourself that a simple, breezy relationship is more solid and permanent than it actually is. Which is what I did.

I think that's one of the most valuable lessons we can learn about relationships: we have to see them for what they actually *are*, not as what we want them to be. As I always say, some people are there for a reason, others for a season. Not everyone is meant to be your partner for a lifetime. Sometimes, things just run their course, and that's okay—or at least it should be.

Well, the relationship with my Omar Sharif happened to run its course right around the time I got the offer to work at *Dateline*. I moved to New York City without him, and that could have been the end of our relationship. For a little while it was. But goodbyes are hard, and being single again isn't always easy—especially when we're bombarded by all these messages telling us that we need to find *the one*, sooner rather than later, and definitely before we're *old*, otherwise we might just die alone. Ha! As if that's the only option. And as if any of us are following the same timeline.

Still, it can be hard to push out all the noise that insists we should do things by a certain date. It's easy to fall into the comparison trap, and I think my Omar Sharif and I both did. We let the idea that *we should be married by now* influence us. So, instead of us taking the opportunity to part ways and stay solo, he came out to visit and proposed during a Central Park horse ride . . . and I said yes.

*Yes, sure, why not, might as well.* That was my thinking. Meaning, I didn't jump into marriage as much as I slipped into it. We were comfortable together, it was time, and it seemed like the logical next step. We'd have a big party with all our friends and family in Punta Cana and just add in a little ol' wedding while we were at it. It would be *fine*.

And for a while it was. But I think we both knew that it wasn't really right for either of us, and it wasn't going to go the distance. I don't regret that time in my life because every experience gets you a little bit closer to where you are today—where you were meant to be. But I bet if you could have paused us midair, as we were slipping into marriage, to ask, *Hey, is this what you really want?* we would have looked at each other and said . . . naaaah.

Sometimes, it feels like our chance to look around has passed. We've said yes to a job that doesn't feel right, committed to an activity that we don't really have time for, or agreed to meet up with friends when we know that what we really need is a quiet night in. And we feel bad for changing our minds, for only looking and considering the situation *after* we committed. And while, sure, it's better if we do all our looking around and thinking *before* we make our decision to say yes, life doesn't always happen that way. So we ignore the voice that says, *Hold up, this doesn't feel right.* Instead, we push it aside, and we worry and stress and lose sleep at night because we don't want to disappoint anyone or let them down. *It's too late, no going back now,* we think. But sometimes it takes courage to admit that just because something ain't broke, it still may not necessarily be working. After all, when we say yes to something for the wrong reasons, we're not letting someone else down, but we're definitely failing ourselves.

It can feel like a big, terrifying jump into the unknown to put ourselves first, but we'll probably have a much smoother and more stable landing if we do. It's never too late to get it right!

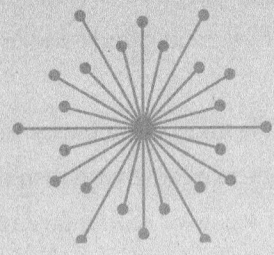

"I wanted a perfect ending. Now I've learned, the hard way, that some poems don't rhyme, and some stories don't have a clear beginning, middle, and end. Life is about not knowing, having to change, taking the moment and making the best of it, without knowing what's going to happen next. Delicious ambiguity."

—Gilda Radner

## Jumpstart

### ALLY LOVE

Ally Love always kicks my butt, and I'm totally down for it. Several times a week, I hop aboard my Peloton stationary bike and happily sweat for an hour, inspired and exhausted by Ally. She's not only a beloved Peloton instructor, she's a model, dancer, *Today* contributor, arena host of the Brooklyn Nets, and founder of the female empowerment company Love Squad. Talk about accomplished! That's why I was surprised to find out that Ally—like so many of us—sometimes falls into the comparison trap.

In 2023, on my podcast, *Making Space*, Ally shared with me how comparing herself to others led to a full-blown confidence crisis.

"The last couple of years, I feel like I lost myself a little bit. I started comparing myself a lot. Social media is just tough. It's tough on kids. It's also tough on adults. I started comparing where I was right now in my career and then in my personal life and looking at all the things I didn't have, not necessarily focusing on what I do have," she said. "I would compare it to where my colleagues are or where people that I followed for years, where they are, and how either I'm not there or they're progressing so much quicker than I am. And I recognized that it was killing my confidence. It was making me immobile."

Ally Love, immobile? It's hard to imagine that anyone as inspiring and motivating as her could feel stuck. She's the very definition of energy and positivity! But she's also human like the rest of us.

Ally said that losing her sense of self in recent years was scary and uncomfortable, so she slowly began to reclaim her identity. She started by giving herself pep talks, even pumping herself up on the way to *Today* appearances.

"You belong there. They like you. They want you there," she said she'd tell herself. "You're here to help other people. This is not for you."

Listening to audiobooks and sermons also helped to ground and reassure her. But it was during a conversation with a friend about the challenges of being 100 percent ourselves that Ally had a breakthrough.

"I said to her, 'So you're worried that Mary Smith, who you don't know, is not going to like the person God made?'" she explained. "And when she looked at me, I realized I was really talking to myself. 'Who am I not to like who God created?'"

Ally said she's now in a better place, and that it's been energizing to embrace a change in her outlook; to embrace who she truly is and what she wants. She said there's power in recognizing that she is enough and that she's doing just fine in life. *Her* life.

Amen! Preach, girl! Way to push through, Ally. Now crank up that music and let's go for a spin!

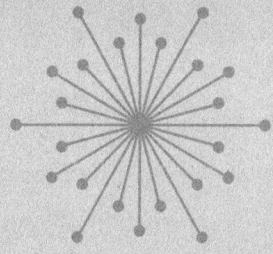

**"Just be yourself, there is no one better."**

—Taylor Swift

# Jumpstart

## THOMAS RHETT

Sometimes it requires real discipline to be quiet, tune out the other voices, and look inward. Who has time for that? Take country superstar Thomas Rhett. When I sat down with him and asked what his perfect day looked like, he mentioned fly-fishing by himself. Having a day just for him, alone, out on the water, in nature, and away from the hustle and bustle of the city and responsibilities of work and parenting and caring for others. I so get it. Who doesn't crave a little me time? But for Thomas, it was more than that. It was the act of picking up his fishing pole and putting down the measuring stick.

"It's just the simple act of throwing a rod in and out of the water," he explained. "There's no one to compare myself to except for myself. I think as awesome as social media can be, I think it ruins a lot of people. And I'm in that box. I mean, shoot, I guess I've had social media for almost ten years now. And I feel like every time I log on to my Instagram account, I get this really quick little rush of like, *Oh my goodness, what did someone say about my song? Or What did they say about this?* But then I see one negative thing, and my day is just ruined. So, when I do get to put my phone down for five or six hours, I find my anxiety level just dropping down and down."

It's crazy how crummy the who-did-it-better game can make us feel. As the saying goes, comparison is the thief of joy. But, we still do it! Throughout the day, we scroll on our devices and peek into the lives of friends, colleagues, and strangers, convinced the lovely snippets they've shared tell their whole story. We see people on far-flung vacations or celebrating major milestones and it can make us feel like we're not measuring up. Instead of feeling inspired, we feel defeated.

Well, how about we quit that? Let's drop the yardstick and only take stock of our own lives. *Is this what I really want or do I want something different? What would it take for me to feel more joy?* If we're going to take some leaps in life, our aim will be so much better if we focus on where *we* want to land, not where someone else has.

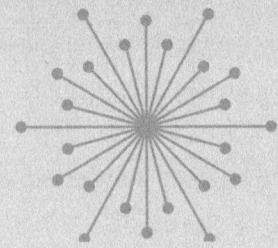

"You are unique. You have different talents and abilities. You don't have to always follow in the footsteps of others. And most importantly, you should always remind yourself that you don't have to do what everyone else is doing and have a responsibility to develop the talents you have been given."

—Roy T. Bennett

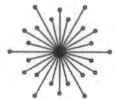

## DON'T BE AFRAID TO CHANGE YOUR STORY

When I was younger, I always assumed motherhood would happen for me. Sure, I was going full throttle in my career, and my relationships were still mostly relegated to that familiar sidecar position, but I just believed I'd be a mom someday. It was a given. But as the years passed, I started wondering if I was subconsciously making decisions that were preventing that role from happening. After all, I really hadn't made much room in my life for motherhood. I was enjoying my job, my family, and my friends. And there were plenty of kids in my life, just none of my own. *Well, I guess motherhood is for other people* was the story I began to tell myself as I entered my forties. And like any story we invent, the more we tell it, the more we believe it. But I'll never forget the day when all of that changed. When the story I'd been telling myself took a turn and set me on the journey to motherhood.

It was a gorgeous, lazy summer day in Southampton. I was strolling with one of my best friends, drinking coffee and catching up. The sun was bright and a warm breeze was coming off the Atlantic. We were talking openly and honestly, the way you can with old friends who truly know you. I think we had just been to another baby shower or kid's birthday party because it was around the time when everyone we knew was having those celebrations. People we saw there were either already parents or on their way there. Everyone, that is, except us.

I remember my friend commenting on it, saying something like, "Yeah, but you and I, we never wanted kids." Wait, what? There was something about hearing her say it out loud that made me stop and realize that her comment was actually not true. In fact, every time I saw someone I loved with a baby I was thrilled for them. I didn't think *Why you and not me?* but I did think, *Why not you* and *me?*

I guess I'd just convinced myself that there must be a reason that I wasn't moving toward becoming a mother. I realized that I'd been wearing this thick suit of armor to all these baby showers, protecting myself from the very idea that I might want children. For years, I'd told myself, *Well, it just isn't a part of my journey,* and *God must have a reason,* and *It will all make sense to me later.* But on that day, walking with my friend, something changed. I turned to her and said, "Actually, I do want to be a mom. I've always wanted to be one."

Whoa. I couldn't believe I'd said it. I'd never admitted it out loud. I'd barely ever admitted it to myself! It was such a surprise—to both of us. My friend was caught off guard. I think we both were. For so long, I'd just thought, *What's the point of saying you want something if you don't believe it's going to happen? Why dwell on what can't be?* But something changed on that sunny day.

And once I'd said it out loud, there was no taking it back. I didn't want to! What a relief and a revelation. And you know what they say, the moment you put something out into the universe, you start seeing signs—everywhere. And I did.

My first sign was reading a story featuring actress Sandra

Bullock. She was my exact age and she'd just adopted a child. I thought, *Oh my gosh, it's possible for me, too!*

Shortly after that, I saw an image on TV of a toddler covered in ash and blood following an airstrike during the Syrian Civil War. My mothering instinct kicked in even harder! There were so many kids out there who needed love and support. Maybe *I* could be that person for a child.

Suddenly, everywhere I turned, I saw possibility and hope. I knew from that moment on that nothing would stop me from becoming a mother.

Haven't you found that sometimes the stories we tell ourselves about our lives aren't true? It's so freeing to think that we can revisit and reevaluate them if needed. Don't be afraid to change yours. If you've got a leap buried inside you—crouched and ready to launch—maybe try this: Say what you want out loud. Even just quietly to yourself. Whisper it into your pillow. Or scream it into the bathroom mirror. Just say it! Now say it louder!

(Uh-huh. I think your leap just heard you.)

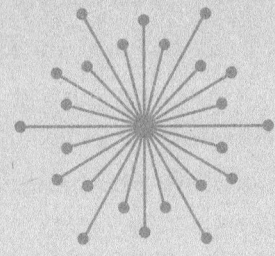

"Change your story, change your life.

Basically, that's what it is."

—Deepak Chopra

## Jumpstart

### MEL ROBBINS

Okay, maybe you've reached the end of this section and you're thinking, *So, now what? I still feel a little stuck.* I get that. Making a change can feel overwhelming, even when we know we need to do it.

There've been a bunch of times in my life when I've looked around and known that I had changes to make, but it felt like I was wearing big ol' cement shoes. I just couldn't move as quickly as I wanted—or even anywhere at all. It's an icky feeling, and maybe you know what I'm talking about. That's why I loved sitting down with motivational speaker and bestselling author Mel Robbins for my podcast in 2023. She's an expert on being stuck because she's experienced that paralyzing, depressing place herself.

"I invented this thing called the five-second rule out of desperation to help me get out of bed," she explained. "I had crushing anxiety because I was eight hundred grand in debt, I had three kids under the age of ten, and I was unemployed."

Gosh, talk about needing a boost to get moving! Mel developed a strategy just to get out of bed. I asked her to describe her five-second rule for any of us who feel stuck or even just uncertain.

"All you do is in a moment when you feel yourself hesitating, procrastinating, beating yourself up, or whatever the old pattern is, just count backward: five, four, three, two, one. And the backward part is critical," she said. "Habit researchers call it a starting ritual—a little hack that's a positive trigger. By the time you get to one, you now have the part of the brain that helps you change, that helps you learn new behavior, that helps you act with courage and confidence, and then you move."

Mel said that any kind of initial forward motion is effective. Volunteer, sign up for a class, start a hobby. Just get out of your head and get moving.

"Any human being can change, period, and stuck doesn't mean you have stopped," she said. "Stuck is a signal wired into your soul and your DNA, and that signal is trying to tell you something very simple. It's trying to tell you that you've stopped growing."

She explained that we're designed to grow and change throughout our entire lives, so it's imperative that we consider being stuck as a call to action, not an existential crisis. When I asked for some ways to rewire our brains, she suggested choosing something to be intentional about each day. Even small stuff, like reading a few chapters of a book or spending time with a friend.

"Studies show it creates a deeper sense of fulfillment and meaning in your life," she said, "because you feel a sense of control, because you're seeing yourself take the actions that are proving to you that yes, in fact, you do come first; yes, in fact, you matter; yes, in fact, I believe in myself; and yes, the things that are important to me are a priority."

Well, heck. Five-four-three-two-one. Eyes closed and I can almost feel those cement shoes turning into a cute pair of sneakers. And, we're off and running!

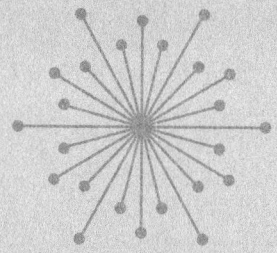

"The way to get started is to quit

talking and begin doing."

—Walt Disney

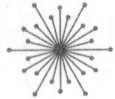

## HELPFUL TIPS AND TOOLS

I find it helps to have a few tools to get the wheels of change turning. A little road map to get me on my way. So over the years, I've come up with several things that work for me. And they're all free!

### Take a Deep Breath

Meditation has been around forever, but I only started doing it in my fifties. In the morning, I light a candle, close my eyes, and get very quiet at my desk. There are lots of different ways to meditate, so experiment with where and how you want to do it. It could be sitting in lotus on the floor for a half hour or just cozying up in your favorite comfy chair for five minutes. Whatever works for you! You're just taking some time to check in with your mind, body, and soul with no outside distractions.

Lately, I've been doing transcendental meditation, repeating a mantra or phrase over and over to quiet my mind. It centers me and gives me energy at the same time. But you don't have to use a mantra. Maybe a phrase resonates with you, like *I am enough*, *I am worthy*, or *I embrace change*. If repeating a phrase isn't your thing, then simply focus on your breath, inhaling and exhaling, really listening to all the sounds around you. The idea is to be still and centered, drop in, and be present. It's a great way to get real about how you're truly feeling.

## Write It Down

For decades now, I've kept a journal. And I admit, it can feel funny at first. *Dear Diary, today I . . .* what? Like, what the heck are you even supposed to put in there? Well, whatever you'd like! This is *your* journal—you can write anything you want! It can be as silly or serious as you're feeling at that moment. I like to say that I'm scribbling in my journal rather than writing in it. It takes the pressure off. And scribbles are just for me; they're not meant to be read by anyone else.

If you're thinking about making a change, journaling can be a great place to start. Take a look around, take stock, and write it down. You could create categories for the main areas that you want to focus on, like work, relationships, family, or whatever *your* focus is. Now write a list of what's working and what brings you joy. Then write another list of things you'd like to change or improve. Look at you! You're journaling!

## Imagine It

Another way to start is to visualize who you would be if you made a change. Feel your joy. Imagine your day. As powerhouse preacher and author Sarah Jakes Roberts says, "If you're going to take a leap, before you even move your feet and put on your shoes, what are you jumping to? The more you can envision, the more discontent you'll feel with the present version of who you are." If you feel stuck and want to make a change, seeing it is the first step toward achieving it.

# Part 2

## Leap of Faith

A leap of faith isn't something you can see; it's a dynamic, invisible act performed in the mind. In a quiet moment, we dream big. We launch ourselves toward some sort of grand change with a vast expanse of the unknown below. And whoops—we've packed our bags so full of promise that there's zero space left for evidence or logic! We just sail through the air feeling terrified, energized, and optimistic—all at the same time.

If you look up the phrase in the dictionary, you'll see a "leap of faith" defined as an "act of believing in something that can't be proved." Right there, in writing, it's warning us: All bets are off. Time to jump. Hope you've got some backup! For some of us, that backup is a higher power. For others, it's a gut feeling that everything's going to work out all right. For many people, maybe it's even a little bit of both!

But there are no guarantees with a leap of faith. No "do *this*, and you'll get *that*" kinds of promises. And maybe that's why so many of us are afraid to shake up our careers, relationships, or personal goals. When we consider doing something that upsets the status quo, the word *doubt* starts flashing in our minds brighter than the red HOT NOW sign at Krispy Kreme doughnuts. But that's to be expected. As psychologist Jim Taylor wrote in *Psychology Today*, "If you didn't have doubts, it wouldn't require a leap of faith."

I think when we're trying to wrap our heads around this life-changing stuff, it's important to point out what a leap of faith is *not*. It's not reckless or impulsive. LOFs (Leap-of-Faithers) don't hang out with SOPs (Seat-of-the-Pantsers). Nope. A leap of faith goes so much smoother when there's careful consideration and planning involved. I like what entrepreneur and writer Sahil Bloom has to say about shortening the enormous "hundred-foot gap" between where you are and where you want to be. Bloom calls it his 30-for-30 approach.

"Carve out 30 minutes per day for 30 straight days to focus on creating evidence for your new path," he suggests. "900 minutes of focused effort should give you a great body of work to start from."

In my own life, I've found that a good plan boosts my confidence, which helps guide me when I want to venture outside my comfort zone. Belief in yourself is a must-have in the leaper's go-bag, but sometimes having others believe in you is a game changer, too. Some of my biggest leaps of faith were launched by others. People who took a chance on me when I really needed it—and boy, am I ever grateful that they did. I'm thankful, too, for the support system I've had during major moves I've made in my life. Family, friends, colleagues, and even people I've never met have served as a loving net beneath me as I've jumped into something new. Change feels less risky when there's a huge pile of pom-poms waiting to break your fall.

So, let's move forward and hear from others who've managed to make a move from point A all the way to point Z. Maybe you'll be inspired as you read about how and why they jumped. They took their shot! After all, in the words of Hockey Hall of Famer Wayne Gretzky, "You miss a hundred percent of the shots you don't take."

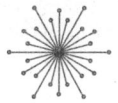

## A SECOND CHANCE TO MAKE A FIRST IMPRESSION

I've never been a fashionista, especially early on in my career when money was tight and no one was guiding me. But I did own a few blazers. I *loved* the way I felt when I slipped on a nice suit jacket: cool, competent, and ready to grind. Still, when I was working at my very first job for WXVT in Greenville, Mississippi—where the great Stan Sandroni hired me—I never imagined that two long sleeves, shoulder pads, and a collar would change the course of my professional life.

I remember the day it happened like it was yesterday. I was at the station working away when Stan suddenly rushed in, huffing and puffing and clearly panicked. By the look on his face, I assumed something terrible must've happened! I prepared myself to hear about a horrible accident or a natural disaster. The last thing I expected to hear him say was, "Who's got a blazer?!"

*Huh? A blazer?* "I do," I said, pointing to where my blazer was hanging up on the back of the office door.

"Great. Because Anne Martin is sick, so you're anchoring the evening news," Stan announced.

*I'm sorry, what? Did my blazer and I just get a promotion? Boy, that was easy!* Or so I thought.

When the time came for me to take my big shot, I put on that blazer, and I prayed—*hard*. My heart was pounding, and I was freaking out. It reminded me of my old days playing basketball at Fort Hunt High School when the buzzer was about to go off and the whole team was counting on me to make the shot. Talk about pressure! Anne Martin was the queen of television news in Greenville, a city staple beloved by viewers. I was the new girl they were just starting to get to know on their TV sets as the Greenwood bureau chief. Thankfully, that night, I had a teleprompter loaded with the exact words I was supposed to say. All I had to do was take a deep breath, relax, and read what was on the screen. How hard could that be?

Apparently, *very*. As the words started to scroll before my eyes, my brain short-circuited, and instead of reading what was written, I smiled into the camera and said, "Good morning, I'm Anne Martin."

What?! Not only did I mess up the time of day, I didn't even get my name right. My own name! What was the matter with me? Now I was in my head, which from that moment on was *not* a good place to be. Every sentence that came out of my mouth contained one stumble and bumble after another. The next thirty minutes of news were atrocious. It turns out a natural disaster *was* happening in Greenville that day, and it was wearing a blazer!

When the newscast mercifully ended, you could've heard a pin drop in the studio. The floor director looked at me like, *OMG, what was that?* Remember, this was a tiny news market— I think we were 168th out of 200 in terms of viewership nationwide—so the audience was small and the stakes were low. Professional train wrecks there were not unheard of. It took *a lot* to rattle the crew in a place like that . . . but I had done it.

The floor director and I just stared at each other, and after a moment of mortifying silence, he walked over, quietly removed my microphone, and held it between his fingers like it was contaminated. I wanted to die. *Well*, I thought, *I guess that's that. I'll just go and collect my pink slip and head home.* But Stan wasn't around to give it to me; maybe he was hiding? I didn't know what was worse—getting fired right now or having to come back the next day for the axe. There was only one thing to do: eat my feelings. I headed to the grocery store and as I roamed the aisles searching for comfort food, a woman turned to me and said, "Oh my Gawd, I just saw you on TV, and I felt *so* sorry for you." *Yeah, you and me both, lady.* I left and went home with my two best friends, Ben & Jerry.

The next day I headed into the news station and went straight to Stan to apologize.

"Well," he said, "I seen what you did, and it was *horrible*. But Anne is still sick, so you might as well put on that blazer and try again."

What? A second chance? I was terrified, but I also wanted so badly to prove to myself—and the lady in the grocery aisle—that I could do better.

And you know what? I did. It was evening, I was Hoda, and the rest is history.

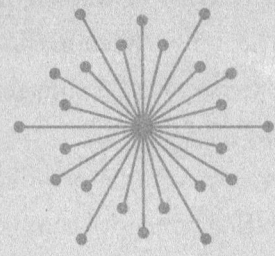

"Don't think there are no second chances.

Life always offers you a second chance.

It's called tomorrow."

—Nicholas Sparks

# Jumpstart

## STEVE HARVEY

Entertainer extraordinaire Steve Harvey knows a lot about grace under pressure, and whether he's on or off the air he's unafraid of laughing or crying. And I love that about him. Maybe because I do a lot of both, too. Known as one of the busiest people in his industry, Steve is an Emmy Award–winning entertainer, radio personality, motivational speaker, *New York Times* bestselling author, businessman, and philanthropist. But, for Steve, busy didn't come easy. He began dreaming about entertaining the masses by ten years old. When I interviewed him in 2023 he was sixty-six, and I was struck by how gutsy he was to fight early on for his authenticity, nearly three decades ago.

"The first year on TV, they told me, 'You talk too country, and if you don't change that, you won't be able to last on television,'" he explained. "I didn't know what to do with that, cuz what else was I gonna be? I don't really have a lot of good grammar in me. This is how I am."

Executives at the time even offered him a linguistics coach, but he turned down the help, committed to taking the leap of faith he'd made to entertain on *his* terms.

"God gives everyone at some point in their life the opportunity to take the shot—to make the decision to go left or right," he said. "I didn't have a Plan B. Everyone I know who had a Plan B had to use it. But, in order to switch your plan, you can't give your all to Plan A."

While Steve said he's experienced his share of challenges along the road to stardom, he credits his success to his mother's prayers and his own perseverance.

"There were a lot of days I didn't think I was gonna make it. There were a lot of days I thought, *Man, this is a bad idea*. But I ain't have another one," he admitted. "I just didn't want to go back home and say I was a failure. I'd already flunked out of college, I'd already messed up my marriage, I'd already lost friends and family members because of my choice."

When I offered that many of us can feel conflicted about our big jumps after we make them, he said, in his experience, hurdles and roadblocks are an important part of our journey.

"If you're going down the path and it feels right, and all of a sudden something starts to go wrong and it doesn't feel right no more, that don't mean nothin'. You got to be tested. You gotta see if you really want it."

Tests and angst came early for Steve. When he quit his day job and pivoted to comedy, he became homeless for three years, sleeping in his car in parking lots. He said at one point he cried out to God, feeling abandoned as he battled to make his dream come true. Then he experienced a divine response.

"I heard, 'If you get up, I'm gonna take you to places you ain't never been,'" he shared.

And get up he did, again and again. Today, the little boy who imagined himself performing in front of ten thousand people now spreads the word about his faith to audiences around the world—a thank-you for his many blessings.

"God never created a soul without giving them a gift. He

put it inside you," he tells people. "You ain't gotta look under the ocean or on a mountain. It ain't under no rocks. It is the thing that you do the absolute best with the least amount of effort. That's your God-given gift. That's the thing you should pursue."

That sure sounds like something to journal about! What is my God-given gift?

"A little more persistence, a little more effort, and what seemed hopeless failure may turn to glorious success."

—Elbert Hubbard

## I NEVER WANT TO WONDER *WHAT IF?*

I'm a big believer that working hard will pay off for you . . . at some point. Through the years, every chance I took in every TV market honed my skills and I got better and better at my job. And you know what? Eventually, after working at six different news stations, the bigwigs at NBC noticed. I felt grateful and proud, but conflicted, too. Believe it or not, the leap of faith required at this point in my career would be one I had to take on myself.

When I was living in New Orleans, I got the call to fly to New York City for a job interview. Elena Nachmanoff, a vice president at NBC News, had seen some of my work and was interested in what I might be able to do at the network level. *The big time.* By this point, I was anchoring the ten o'clock news for WWL TV in New Orleans—the number 42 news market in the country—and I loved my job at the station. My colleagues and I were close, like a family, and as one of the senior anchors at WWL, I had my pick of all the top juicy stories. And I *really* loved New Orleans. It was—and still is —a living, breathing place, and it will always be special to me. When you love that city, it loves you back, and I've *never* met people like New Orleanians—I adore them.

One of my favorites was Frank Davis—chef, sportsman,

and on-air superstar at WWL. He coined the tagline "Naturally N'Awlins" and embodied every bit of that catchy phrase. You'd always see Frank dancing at the Mardi Gras parade or feeding people something down-home and damn good. "C'mon, Hoda, let's go fishin'!" he'd say, his eyes dancing. Or, "You don't eat crawfish like that, Hoda!" Then he taught me how. That city is full of Franks, and I was hooked from day one.

When the call came from NBC, I was in the middle of contract renegotiations with WWL. Mine was nearly up, and I was getting ready to re-sign for multiple years. I had a little window of time before I'd have to renew, so off I went to New York for an interview at the legendary 30 Rockefeller Center. That famous building was just as impressive as everyone said it was. Standing at the entrance looking up, it appeared to be about a thousand stories high! I was meeting with the folks at *Dateline*, the prime-time show I was being considered for, and they couldn't have been nicer. After I was introduced to everyone, we took a tour, and then I went through the interview process. At the end of it all, I got a very warm "Thanks for coming" and headed back home to New Orleans. That whole day was amazing and more than a little surreal, but when a week passed with no word from the network brass, I supposed nothing was going to come of it. I decided to chalk it up as a really cool experience.

But then, the phone rang. It was Elena, calling to explain that the executives at NBC liked me . . . but they weren't sure I could make the jump from local TV (where stories typically run about two minutes long) to *Dateline* (where episodes can run a full hour). They wanted to see me again, but this time, they were giving me homework. They wanted me to cover and write a long, in-depth story, and they were giving me a producer and two crews to make it happen.

At this point in my career, I *had* only written two-minute-long pieces, so they were right to question whether I was up to the task! But I knew I was. A quiet inner voice was telling me *this* was my time to jump, and I was ready to bring all my experience, knowledge, and determination to make it happen.

The story I was asked to report on was complicated; I was interviewing a guy who believed that he was the victim of a fraudulent speed trap in front of the Bronx Zoo. Convinced the cops were tampering with the red lights to ensnare innocent motorists, this man was suing the city, and I was to interview him and a representative from the mayor's office. For *Dateline*, a show watched by more than fifty million viewers each week! I got my interviews, collected my research, and went back to my hotel, where I was given twenty-four hours to pull everything together into a clear, coherent, interesting story. Well, let me tell you, I didn't sleep. I took four showers, drank a ton of coffee, and wrote throughout the night. To quote the great Lin-Manuel Miranda, I was not throwing away my shot.

The next morning, I took my *Dateline* tryout piece back to 30 Rock. Honestly, I wasn't sure if it was genius or if I'd turned in a truly terrible piece of work—I'd lost all perspective. I was ready to view it with the bosses and hear their verdict when something I'd never predicted occurred—breaking news. The world was learning that Mother Teresa had died, which brought everything to a halt. Suddenly, it was all hands on deck at *Dateline* and time for me to go back to NOLA. My story—and the decision about my potential future at NBC—would have to wait.

Back home, I told my bosses that I needed a bit more time

to think about my contract. We agreed that I would get them my answer "soon," although I really had no idea when that would be. A day? A week? A month? The waiting was stressful. A few days later, the call finally came. The NBC executives wanted me back in New York City to screen my piece for *Dateline*.

Well, talk about intimidating. There I was, sitting in a room with a group of senior producers, each with a red pen in one hand and my script in the other. As they watched my story, they scribbled notes all over my script. The more they scribbled, the more nervous I got—and the more I started to second-guess the work I'd done. By the time it was over, I was convinced it had been a disaster and that my piece was total garbage. I thought to myself, *They called me back to watch this slop?* Torture. What's worse, when it was all done, I still didn't have an answer about the *Dateline* job. Were they going to hire me or not? Meanwhile, my bosses back in New Orleans were getting anxious for me to sign my contract. I felt pulled in a million different directions. But something in me said, *Give it a few more days. Don't rush.*

I was sitting at home when Elena Nachmanoff finally called.

"Hoda, you got it."

Got it? What did she mean? "Put it in a full sentence," I said. I needed to be certain.

"You're a correspondent at *Dateline NBC*."

Wow! I couldn't believe it. My blazers and I were headed for the Big Apple! I immediately called my mom, who was working at the Library of Congress.

"Guess what, Mom?" I said. "Your daughter is a correspondent at *Dateline NBC*!" Immediately, I heard my mom yelling the news to her colleagues. I knew where all of them sat. I could picture their big smiles and I could hear them cheering alongside her and celebrating with me. I was so grateful! All that support was just what I needed because what I had to do next would be excruciating—saying goodbye to WWL and New Orleans.

As hard as it was, one of the biggest factors in my decision to move on was never wanting to wonder *What if?* What if I never tried? Clearly, I had no guarantees that I would love working at NBC. And it was hard to leave behind the city, friends, and amazing job I cherished in New Orleans—to start over again at age thirty-three in New York. But I knew that if I *didn't* take the opportunity—to experience a new city, a new station, new colleagues, new expectations and challenges—I would regret it.

It was time to go because it was time to grow.

When I shared my decision at work, some people told me stories about folks they knew who left local news and belly-flopped at the network. The stories went like, *Hey, you remember what happened to so-and-so? They went from being a big fish in a small pond to swimming with sharks!*

I get why folks did this. For one thing, they wanted me to be sure I was making the right decision. But I think another reason was that when people watch someone else make a change and fail, it reinforces their *own* decision not to make a change and instead stay right where they are. *See? Better to sit tight.* It's human nature to want to feel safe and settled.

Yes, change *is* risky! I still remember how dicey that move was for me. For starters, there was a clause in my contract that said the network would reserve the right to fire me after six months if they didn't think I was living up to their expectations. *Gulp.* Then there was the fact that I was going to be starting all over. Small fish in a big pond? I was more like a guppy! At *Dateline*, I was by far the worst in the group when I started. I had a lot to learn. I felt like a junior getting to play with the varsity team. Thankfully, I had some great colleagues who remembered what it's like to be the rookie.

Neal Shapiro truly believed in me and encouraged me to work on my voice so my stories didn't all sound the same. Keith Morrison told me that *his* secret to voicing a story was to pretend like he was reading a bedtime story to his kid. I loved that. I took all the great advice I could get. I still do! But that first year or two wasn't easy. I was grinding away, doing everything possible to keep up. It simply took time for me to find my footing, but eventually I did, and my learning curve was filled with lessons. Covering the horror and humanity of Hurricane Katrina in my beloved New Orleans drove home the value of approaching every story as if it were unfolding in your backyard. I was honored to cover a story called "The Education of Ms. Groves," which took a year to complete. We followed a teacher throughout her first year with the Teach for America program—nothing flashy or titillating. But when we won multiple prestigious awards for that reporting, it reminded me that even a day-in-the-life story can make people feel something.

My leap of faith from the Big Easy to the Big Apple turned out to be the right decision, and I loved both where I had been and where I went. Then and now, the risk of failure will always outweigh the risk of regret for me. Instead of wondering *What if?* I ask *Why not?*

"And, when you want something, all the universe

conspires in helping you achieve it."

—Paulo Coelho

# Jumpstart

### INA GARTEN

Any fan of TV celebrity and cookbook author Ina Garten knows that her loving relationship with her husband of more than fifty years is the key ingredient to her happiness. But that doesn't mean there weren't some lumps in the gravy along the way, some what-ifs in their love story. Within her book *Be Ready When the Luck Happens*, Ina describes her childhood as bleak and lonely. But the very first chapter is about Jeffrey—not her family. When I asked Ina why, she explained that meeting him was when her life began. When, for the first time, she felt "seen" as a person.

"When I met Jeffrey, he was just the opposite. To him, everything I thought was brilliant! Everything I wanted to do was just a brilliant idea," she said. "He just took total delight in me. He made me feel so smart and funny and thoughtful and wonderful, and he was, too."

In 1968, young twenty-year-old Ina and twenty-two-year-old Jeffrey were married. The couple took a whirlwind trip through Europe, where Ina fell in love with French food and began to cook. The pair then moved to Washington, DC, where both began working for the government. At home, Ina continued to hone her cooking skills and started to yearn for a more creative career. By 1978, she quit her job and took a leap of faith to buy a specialty grocery store in the Hamptons called the Barefoot Contessa. The transition was both demanding and exhilarating. Learning and growing the business consumed Ina, and before long, her professional jump would lead to a personal one, too. She began to wonder, *What if I'm not allowed to evolve?*

"I think the girl that Jeffrey married was growing," she said. "As a couple he was the husband and I was the wife, so I would take care of the house and the laundry and cook dinner, and I think as the women's movement was sifting into our consciousness, I began to resent those roles."

So, ten years into their marriage, Ina took another jump—*away* from the love of her life.

"We took a walk on the beach, and I just said to him, 'I need to be on my own for a little while,'" she explained. "And what made it even harder is he said, 'If you feel like you need to be on your own, you need to be on your own.'"

While she stayed in Westhampton and buried herself in work, Jeffrey returned to DC and didn't come back. While Ina says it was scary telling the person she loved deeply that she wasn't happy, she stood by her decision.

"I wanted a partner. I didn't want to be the wife and I didn't want him to be the husband," she said. "I couldn't quite get that message through, so I thought I'd just put on the brakes."

When the store closed for the winter, Ina moved back to DC just as Jeffrey was headed for a long work trip. When he returned, they met in California and talked about what they both needed to stay together.

"He said, 'I'd like to travel more, but because I'm responsible for you, I feel like I can't,'" she explained. "I said, 'You're not responsible for me; we're responsible for each other, and you can.' And he changed his life."

For Ina, she found that once their new partnership was established, any resentment she'd been feeling disappeared.

"Turns out I love making dinner," she said, laughing. "I just didn't want someone to *expect* me to make dinner. We reintroduced ourselves to each other on a different basis, and I remember thinking, *Oh my God, I'm falling in love with somebody who happens to be my husband.*"

Stepping back—or jumping away—to reevaluate our life can be scary! Thank you, Ina, for sharing how making space paid off in such a meaningful way for you and your beloved Jeffrey.

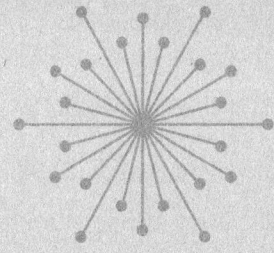

**"Sometimes good things fall apart so**

**better things could fall together."**

*—Marilyn Monroe*

# Jumpstart

## NOELLE BARILLE

Life can be so busy—so noisy—that we don't always have the time or space to ask ourselves how we're feeling. Or to listen to the answer. In 2024, Jenna and I spoke with Noelle Barille, a woman who described her experience with ignoring what her gut was trying to tell her.

"The universe will give you a whisper, it will knock on your door," she said, "and then it will hit you with a brick."

Or, in Noelle's case, a cutting board. She never dreamed that cooking would change her life until her "perfect" world began to crumble.

In her twenties, Noelle said, she began to build a future she thought was solid and secure. "I followed what was expected of me. I got a corporate job, I got married, I did all the things," she explained, "but I didn't think about what I wanted or what my soul was telling me I wanted."

By age thirty, Noelle's marriage was in shambles and her health was failing. Desperate to heal in all ways, she got a divorce and began creating healthy recipes. Before long, her relationship with food and cooking sparked a passion that fueled her hunger for a more rewarding life. In a leap of faith, Noelle quit her corporate job and enrolled in the Culinary Institute of America.

"People literally thought I was crazy," she said. "I was single, I moved to the Hudson Valley where I didn't know anybody, and I enrolled in school, where I was one of the older people on campus," she said. "I remember in a class, a chef came up behind me when I was working on my knife skills and he said, 'My grandmother can cut faster than you,' but I was in heaven. I loved it! I get goose bumps when I think about my time walking on that campus."

After graduating from culinary school, Noelle moved to Italy and began working as a chef instructor on Oceania and Regent Seven Seas cruises. Now, at fifty-four, Noelle says traveling the world and sharing her passion for food is thrilling.

"Part of what is such a gift about the life I've built for myself is that I get to learn about cultures all over the world through the lens of food and cooking," she said. "I think if you live true to your soul and you can get quiet and you can listen to that inner voice inside, you're going to have a fruitful life."

That certainly sounds like a recipe for success, Noelle!

"Intuition doesn't tell you what you want to hear;

it tells you what you need to hear."

—Sonia Choquette

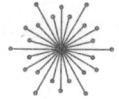

## SURRENDERING CONTROL

I love tennis, and when it comes to leaps of faith, sometimes the ball's in your court, sometimes it's not. Most of us prefer the control that comes with determining our next move, but that's just not how the "match" always works in life. If you've ever been really sick, or experienced illness alongside a loved one, you know what it's like to watch and wait. It's unnerving. At the same time you're praying to God, you're also poring over the plan of attack laid out by trained professionals and relying on well-intentioned people (who might at this point be complete strangers to you) to comfort and heal you. And you're in shock. Talk about the ball being in the other court.

I experienced all these emotions when I was diagnosed with breast cancer in 2007 at the age of forty-three. I'd been at *Dateline* for nearly nine years at that point, and after a rough start (and a heck of a lot of hard work), I finally felt like things had fallen into place with my professional life. Producers were sending me all over the globe to cover stories, and I loved my colleagues and the collaboration we engaged in to turn out our very best work. The news business was and always will be fast and furious, so I controlled the things I could—getting to the airport early, having double the notes for background research, not waiting to tape an interview. While everything was spinning around me, I looked for things I could steady.

Then, out of the blue, I was diagnosed with cancer—a life-and-death situation that was *completely* out of my control. As you might imagine, this sometime control freak had more than a little trouble handing over power and accepting just how little say she had in what came next. My sister, Hala, immediately put her life on hold and moved in with me. She went to every single medical appointment, a second set of eyes and ears. Still, even with her by my side, I felt helpless. You know when you're riding in a friend's car, and you reflexively try to hit the brakes if they get a little too close to the car in front of you, even though you're not the one behind the wheel? That was me, slamming my foot on a nonexistent pedal, trying to control the cancermobile.

Ironically, at the same time I was pumping the brakes, everything about the situation felt so urgent. *I have to get a doctor* right now! *I need to do the surgery* ASAP! *Come on, people, let's get on it!* But the folks who diagnosed me advised me to hold up. They said I had time to search for not just *a* doctor, but the right doctor. And thank God I listened. I found not only the right doctor but the best surgeon I could've asked for.

Turns out, I was just beginning to learn what surrender felt like.

The one thing I did have control of at this crazy time was when and with whom I shared the news of my diagnosis. It was a secret I guarded for a time, letting almost no one into my circle of trust. That included the people I worked with, especially the higher-ups. I guess I felt that even if I didn't have much power over what was happening to my health, I could still control who knew about it. But soon I had to let go of that, too. I needed time off from work to make a plan and get the care I needed. So, feeling weak and vulnerable, my heart pounding, I made an appointment with my boss at the time, David Corvo, and asked for a leave of absence. When he asked if everything was okay, I broke down. I told him through tears that I had breast cancer and needed a mastectomy. I hated saying it and hearing myself say it.

Still, I'll never forget what David told me that day. He said, "I know a lot of people who've had breast cancer, and they all have one thing in common—they're still here."

What an amazing gift he gave me—hope backed by hard facts. It took a lot of surrender to have that conversation with David that day. Being vulnerable wasn't easy, and it didn't come naturally to me, especially back then. But sometimes, when you find the courage to take a leap of faith and share a hard truth, you're blessed with words of true comfort. *They're still here.* Thank you, David. By the grace of God, so am I.

I feel the same gratitude toward my angel in the operating room, Dr. Freya Schnabel. At every step of the way, Freya was endlessly kind and reassuring, both with me and—crucially—with my loved ones, who were understandably even more terrified than I was. I recall that just as I was getting ready to be wheeled into surgery, I looked at who was beside me—my mom. She was amazing during that time and with me every step of the way. I knew that at that very moment, she was suffering even more than I was. I'll never forget the desperate look in her eyes. There she was, having to entrust her kid to a complete stranger. Ugh, I know that was so hard for her. My mom was crying, and Freya paused and addressed her directly, calmly saying, "Don't worry; we're going to take care of your little girl." As comforted as she could possibly be by those reassuring words, my mom watched as they rolled me into the operating room. Then, we all took a leap of faith—we had no other choice.

"Faith is unseen but felt; faith is strength when we feel

we have none, faith is hope when all seems lost."

—Catherine Pulsifer

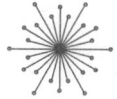

## THOSE FOUR FABULOUS WORDS

There's nothing like a near-death experience to remind you just how precious life is. After the surgery was over and I was at home healing, I had a peaceful start to my recovery. (Or maybe that was just all the painkillers I was on.) But one morning, I literally shot up in bed, wide awake, the fog of recovery completely gone. Somehow, a powerful string of words had been presented to me. I don't know if they were my own or if they were sent from God. Whatever the case, I heard this simple phrase in my head, clear as day: *You can't scare me.*

Boom! My perspective on life had just been completely transformed. It's like that proverbial tennis ball had bounced onto the court right in front of me, and I could fire it back over the net and make it land *wherever* I wanted it to. I was once again in control, but now in a more a positive, freeing way. Clearly, I'd already faced the scary thing *and* I'd lived through it. I was alive! What could possibly intimidate me after I'd survived cancer? Suddenly, I felt bolder and braver, like I had nothing to lose and everything to gain. That's when the new me began to consider what she really wanted at NBC.

Keep in mind that until that moment I had always sat quietly and minded my own business on the job. I was a hard worker; I knew that and felt confident in my skills. I just figured that the higher-ups would notice me and appreciate my contributions, and that eventually I'd get rewarded without ever having to ask for it. Time for a promotion? Great, I'll just be right over here at my desk waiting for one. The first one into the office and the last one to leave, that's me. I'm over here! Hmm. Still here . . . at my desk. Just waiting, and waiting, and . . . what the heck was I waiting *for*?! Asking for a promotion may have been scary before cancer, but after cancer? Bring it on.

My mindset now was, *Who cares? Who gives a rip?* I was going to ask for what I wanted because I knew more than ever that my life had a beginning and an end. That was the first time it hit me. I wondered, *What do I really want professionally?* I'd been at NBC for nine years, and I was done being careful and polite. No more waiting to be noticed.

So, I mustered up all my courage and decided to go to the fifty-second floor of 30 Rock—home to the NBC executive offices—and pitch myself for the new fourth hour of *Today*. If the answer was no, it was no. I will admit, the whole elevator ride up my heart was pounding and I was sweating. This was a leap of faith of the highest order with the CEO of NBC-Universal.

But, oddly, the moment I got into Jeff Zucker's office, I was suddenly calm. I took my time and explained to Jeff that now that I'd recovered from cancer, I was different. I wasn't the same Hoda Kotb they'd known as a buttoned-up anchor at *Dateline* for all those years—or at least, that wasn't *all* of me. That wasn't all I could do.

The words were pouring out of me. And for the first time, though it was still a bit terrifying, I asked for something in my professional life.

"I want that job on the fourth hour of *Today*," I said. "I think I'd be good at it. I know you see me a certain way, but I can do this, and . . ." And then I started crying and I couldn't stop!

Jeff was probably thinking, *You're different, all right.* But I knew that he had gone through cancer himself, so when I was done blubbering and talking, I asked him if he'd experienced that same feeling of fearlessness after he'd recovered.

He smiled and said, "Every day."

I do wonder sometimes why it took a severe illness for me to start asking for what I wanted. Maybe it was because I was so conditioned to say thank-you, to accept what I'd been given, and to just feel lucky. I thought I had all the time in the world, right? But when I realized that I didn't—that none of us do—the fearlessness that was always inside me finally found its voice.

And I got the promotion.

"The only way to find your voice is to use it."

—Jen Mueller

# Jumpstart

### CHIP CONLEY

Remember Chip Conley? He's the guy I told you about earlier who's working to rebrand middle age. Well, during that same conversation, he shared a story about how facing death changed his perspective on life, too. And in quite an other-worldly way.

Chip said that when he was forty-seven, he broke his ankle playing baseball during a friend's bachelor party. When a bacterial infection developed in his leg, he was prescribed drugs to cure it.

"I was put on an antibiotic and it was way too strong," he explained. "And I died after giving a speech onstage."

Chip died! While signing books after a 2008 speech in St. Louis, he blacked out and his heart stopped beating. He was later told that he'd flatlined nine times over the next ninety minutes. Nine. Times. I asked Chip if he remembered anything about what he called "going to the other side."

"I was in a mountain chalet on the second floor with a high ceiling and a skylight," he described. "The light was beautiful, and there were blue skies, and I could hear birds everywhere."

Chip said the walls of the chalet were washed in a rainbow pattern, and that everything was moving very slowly around him. On the ground, he noticed a tropical-scented oil flowing lightly along the wooden floor and down the stairs. He was in complete awe, a feeling that stayed with him when he finally came back to life.

"What I took from that was to slow down and to actually just appreciate the beauty of life, and to be in a state of awe," he said. "I kept thinking, *I don't feel a state of awe very much in my life.* And so, when I left the hospital two days later, I said, 'I've gotta change everything.'"

And he did. With the goal of furthering his sense of wonder, Chip took a leap of faith and sold the boutique hotel chain he'd started at age twenty-six.

"I was selling it at the worst time in the market," he said, "but I just knew that this wasn't what I was supposed to be doing."

That freedom led to a position as Airbnb's head of global hospitality and strategy. Then, at fifty-seven, Chip cofounded the Modern Elder Academy, which you read about earlier, proof that it's never too old for a transformation!

"Midlife is a time where we start to shed the identities and the showing off," he said. "Just show up. Don't worry about showing off, show up."

I gotta say, Chip, I'm in awe of you. Not only do you show up, but your energy, ability to adapt, and positive outlook on growing older fans the flames for any of us looking to get fired up for what's next. *Awesome!*

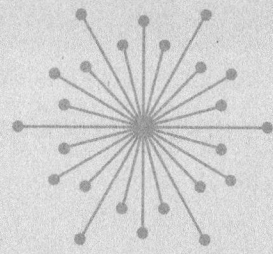

"If you don't make the time to work on creating the life

you want, you're eventually going to be forced to spend

a lot of time dealing with a life you don't want."

—Kevin Ngo

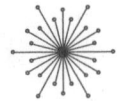

## DON'T HOG YOUR JOURNEY

As you may know firsthand, a near-death experience or a health scare completely terrifies you, but it teaches you things, too. Welcome each day as it comes. Be open to new people and experiences. Don't take everything so seriously. And that comfort zone you're so cozy in? Step out of it. I'll bet you could add some of your own lessons here, too. Unexpectedly, one of the most impactful teaching moments for me following breast cancer unfolded in midair.

Once I'd battled the disease with support from my family and close friends and told a few people at NBC, well, that was enough. I just wanted to get beyond it. Forward! I went back to work as soon as I could, although, in hindsight, probably a little too soon.

In 2007, just two months after my surgery, I was on a plane coming back from Ireland after shooting a segment called "Where in the World Is Matt Lauer?" I was exhausted. All I wanted to do was recline my seat, put in my earplugs, and get some sleep. But my chatty seatmate had no intention of letting that happen. Ken Duane, an affable business executive whom I later affectionately dubbed the Man on the Plane, had other ideas. He wanted to talk.

Ken asked about my show, my colleagues, how my bosses viewed my work, and how I defined myself. So much for small talk, Ken! But he was friendly and likable, and we got to chatting. Well, you know how sometimes you find yourself telling things to a stranger you wouldn't normally tell anyone else? It was like that with him. So, when Ken asked me what kind of procedure I'd had that required the compression sleeve I was wearing, I told him what I'd been hiding from so many other people in my life (and our viewers, too).

"I'm recovering from surgery for breast cancer," I explained.

There, I'd said it. But I also didn't want Ken—or anyone—to define me by it. *That news lady with breast cancer.* I told him that I hoped he'd think of at least five other things about me before he thought about the breast cancer. In my mind, there was me, and then there was the cancer. I didn't want us to be one and the same. That's when Ken said something surprising.

"What's wrong with you? Breast cancer is a part of you." He said that my experience with cancer was as much a part of me as college, work, or anything else in my life I'd lived through. He didn't see it as something I needed to hide. I'll never forget what he suggested next: "Don't hog your journey. It's not just for *you.*"

Wow, that really stuck with me. *Don't hog your journey.* Encouraging me further, he said, "Sure, you could take your cancer journey to your grave. Or you could share your story, in the hopes that it might help someone else."

I thought a lot about that thirty-thousand-foot conversation in the days and weeks that followed. Maybe Ken was right. I wrestled with whether to take a big leap of faith and share something so personal about my life with the whole world.

But months later, during National Breast Cancer Awareness Month, that's exactly what I did. It was surreal. Now I was the one being interviewed, sitting down with Ann Curry for a special *Today* segment. Part of it was videotaped prior to our live on-set conversation.

"So, you're mourning a couple of things. You're mourning the loss of what was your body," Ann said to me.

"Yeah. Some days I'm in the shower and I'm like, *Jesus. My God. I'm so upset.* And some days I'm thinking, *Hold on a second. You got your life back. And if this is the scar that shows it, embrace it.*"

Ann gently said, "So you're thinking about who you once were; that sort of carefree girl is gone."

I agreed but told her I felt different and better. Stronger than I felt before. We talked about my not being able to have children, and then the videotaped portion of the interview ended.

When the red light lit up on the in-studio cameras, I knew we were now broadcasting live . . . and I lost it. I started blubbering and choking out the story of the man on the plane, explaining the reason I was sitting there, vulnerable and emotional. The segment was difficult, but thankfully, as scary as it was to share my story that day, Ken was right. Viewers around the country had tuned in to my interview, and the response was amazing. We heard from countless people going through their own cancer journeys, as well as from the loved ones of friends and family members who'd been touched by the disease. For some folks, my experience was a reminder that they weren't alone.

One viewer emailed: *Thank you for sharing the personal details, as the disfigurement part of our disease is a huge part of the battle. Thank you for saying if they are the scars to be alive, then great! That's a new way of looking at all my scars when I just feel so ugly because of them.*

For others, my story was a reminder to schedule their mammograms!

Emails like this one poured in: *My mother is a two-time survivor of breast cancer, as is my sister-in-law. Despite this, I have been too busy to make my mammogram appointment. When I saw your segment, I jumped up off the couch and ran to the phone. Staying alive needs no excuse. Thank you, thank you, thank you.*

Incredible! I felt honored and humbled by the overwhelming response—and honestly, a little undeserving. Many people had gone through what I'd been through and *worse.* I was fortunate to have excellent medical care, a great job to return to, and a wonderful support system of friends and loved ones. Still, cancer is difficult even in the "best" circumstances and it had drained me, just as it does every single person it touches. I hoped my honesty would help others realize that cancer—or any challenge we face—is something that shapes us but doesn't define us. And why not share our journeys and what we've learned along the way? Ken taught me that.

"Your heartache is someone else's hope. If you make it through, somebody else is going to make it through. Tell your story."

—Kim McManus

## Jumpstart

### DELIA EPHRON

For award-winning author and screenwriter Delia Ephron, taking a leap of faith to say her dream out loud took many years . . . and it didn't go well. When I interviewed her in 2022, she told me first about her childhood. She said that she and her sisters—including famed wordsmith Nora Ephron—were raised by parents who were very successful contract writers for 20th Century Fox. Their mother encouraged them to pursue careers, but Delia says she had a different plan after watching the movie *Seven Brides for Seven Brothers* when she was ten years old. In the 1954 film, actress Jane Powell's character quickly marries a lumberjack, moves to the backwoods, and cooks for him and his six brothers.

"And all I wanted to do was get married and make flapjacks for someone," Delia said. "I saw that movie sixteen times, and I learned the power of a romantic comedy very young."

In her twenties, becoming a writer felt daunting to Delia, since Nora and her parents were already extremely successful. So, at twenty-five, she jokingly says, she married "the first man who asked her." Delia moved with him to Rhode Island, where she started a crocheting business. But during a trip to New York, she met an editor at a party and pitched him an idea for an instructional book. It turns out, Simon & Schuster loved the concept, and they published Delia's first book, *The Adventurous Crocheter*, to acclaim shortly thereafter. Once her second book, *Glad Rags* (detailing how to make clothes), was published, Delia told her husband that she wanted to make writing her career.

"And you know how important it is to speak a dream out loud," she shared. "But he said, 'I don't want you to be a writer.' When I asked why, he said, 'Suppose you become famous. I don't want you to become famous.'"

When Delia heard herself promise him that fame would never happen for her, she knew it was time to get a divorce.

"If someone wants to crush your dreams with his big fat foot," she said, "you'd just better get out."

So, knowing that she'd be on her own and competing with her family's success, Delia took a leap of faith and chose to take her shot at writing full-time. Her plan was to give herself two years in New York, with the goal of getting published in *The New York Times*. In 1978, with her deadline nearing and five hundred dollars to her name, inspiration presented itself in the form of homemade chocolate pudding.

"I was eating it *my* way," she described, "y'know, the type you cook, and it has skin on top. And I was scooping the pudding out from underneath it, saving the skin for last. And I thought, *I'm eating like a child.*"

That experience prompted Delia to write a five-hundred-word piece about how kids eat food. Not only did the *Times* pick it up for the Sunday magazine, she was immediately offered a book deal. *How to Eat Like a Child: And Other Lessons in Not Being a Grown-up*, a bestseller, confirmed that changing the course of her life was the right decision.

Delia would go on to write more books and also screenplays, including two blockbusters with Nora: *You've Got Mail* and *The Sisterhood of the Traveling Pants*. In 2022, she released *Left on Tenth: A Second Chance at Life*. It's a beautiful book about losing Nora and her second husband to cancer, managing her own cancer diagnosis, and finding love again at age seventy-two. When I asked Delia about her unexpected later-in-life romance, she simply glowed, telling me how she and Peter Rutter had briefly dated five decades ago, but then reconnected when he reached out after reading her op-ed in the *Times* following her husband's death.

"It was the most charming note, just lovely. And so, of course, I sent it to at least three girlfriends to see what they thought," she said, "because, at that point, I wasn't leaving the house without calling a friend to see if it was a good idea."

And boy, was it ever. The pair fell in love just as she was diagnosed with leukemia, they married in the hospital during her first week of cancer treatments, and they've been at each other's sides since 2017.

"Peter says we weren't meant to be together when we were young," she said, "and that we met when we were supposed to. And I believe that's true."

Oh, finding such deep love later in life. I gotta say, Delia, that's even more inspiring than homemade chocolate pudding.

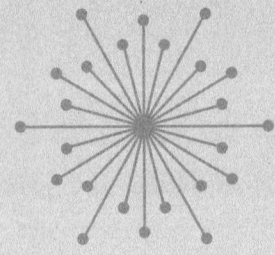

**"Have enough courage to trust love one more**

**time and always one more time."**

—Maya Angelou

## BARING IT ALL

If I'm lucky enough one day to find deep love, I'll be much more confident than I was years ago. Back then, I had some hang-ups. Yes, I'd finally bared my soul to the world about my cancer journey, but the thought of revealing my physical scars to a partner freaked me out. I was so self-conscious. My new body was disfigured, and only my doctor and the kind nurse who'd helped me wash after my procedure had seen it. I could barely handle looking at *myself* in the early days after my surgery—how could I ever expect anyone else to?

When I felt vulnerable, I told myself to be grateful, too. That I'd survived cancer, and, well, being a scarred-up human was just the price I had to pay. If that meant never wearing certain clothes, or a swimsuit, or even *dating* again . . . so be it. I just assumed that a whole part of my life was now over.

I think that's a common reaction for many women who've had a mastectomy: feeling like something has been stripped away. Even if, like me, you're not someone who spends a lot of time thinking about your body, it still impacts you. I knew that being intimate with another person meant that, at some point, they were going to see my reconstructed breast. But I *never* expected that person to be my friend's aunt Harriet!

Harriet was eighty at that time of this encounter. She was the aunt of my friend Jen, and was super cool and artsy—one of those women who's just all-around inspiring to spend time with. A renowned fashion designer, she was always impeccably dressed, with a dazzling smile and a sparkle in her hazel eyes. She was a gray-haired dynamo! One day, we were sitting on the couch at a get-together, and she said that she'd heard I'd had a mastectomy. When I confirmed that I had, she said, simply: "Let me see it."

*Whoa, Harriet.* This was months and months after my surgery, but still *no one* had seen my breast yet. I told her I was nervous. Harriet immediately took my hand and said, "Come with me." She led me into a bathroom and closed the door behind us. I looked at her like she was crazy. I thought, *Does she really think I'm going to show her my boob? No way, not happening.*

Well, before I knew it, she'd lifted up her shirt and showed me *her* knockers! Turns out, Harriet had had a mastectomy in the days before doctors did any kind of reconstruction. Pointing to her chest, she said, "Not so bad, right?" She lowered her shirt and waited. I looked at this brave woman, took a deep breath, and counted three, two, one. Then I lifted up my shirt. Harriet looked at me, shrugged, and said, "Not so bad."

After I covered back up, she asked, "How did that feel? Was it scary?"

Yes, it was scary! It was *terrifying.* But it was such a big moment! It was more than just someone seeing me naked—it was someone helping me get rid of the shame. I had nothing to be ashamed of. I had nothing to hide. That wild and unexpected leap of faith—flashing Harriet!—was a big step toward accepting my post-surgery body.

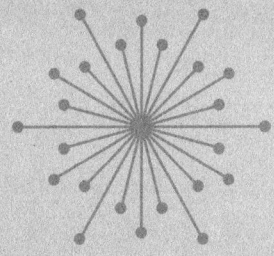

"Courage starts with showing up and

letting ourselves be seen."

—Brené Brown

# Jumpstart

## VIOLA DAVIS

Those bad feelings I once had about my body were so powerful and debilitating. Unfortunately, shame is something we've all felt at one time or another, and of all the emotions, it's one of the crummiest. So we tend to bury it. We're desperate to silence it. As bestselling author and psychology professor Brené Brown writes, "Shame derives its power from being unspeakable." Which is why I think speaking up is so important. When we do, we're not only helping ourselves but we may just help others, too. It's brave *and* inspiring. In her 2022 memoir, *Finding Me*, actress Viola Davis writes about her battle with shame, plus so many other relatable topics that I nearly burned through a yellow highlighter trying to capture them all. When I spoke with this superstar of stage and screen on my podcast, I asked Viola what it felt like to share her personal journey with the world.

"It's terrifying. I'm putting my life out there for the world to judge and observe," she said. "It's like that old saying, 'I know what I said; I just don't know what you heard.'"

Despite the fear, Viola decided to bare it and share it all—to take a huge jump and document her difficult start growing up in Central Falls, Rhode Island. She writes about being starved for a peaceful home life and for food.

"The thing about being hungry is you don't think about anything else," she explained. "You get to school at eight, by eight fifteen, you're falling asleep. Your brain chemistry changes. How you see the world changes, and the worst part is the deep, deep shame."

Viola describes how, as a child, she would ask strangers for money, visit soup kitchens, and make friends with kids who had food at home. Her anxiety grew even worse when boys who didn't look like her started calling her horrible names.

"What I learned from an early age was that I was born into a world that I just didn't fit into," she said. "And I did not have the language to understand the power of being dark-skinned. The potency of being different. Instead, I felt worthless."

Her bleak existence also included domestic violence at home. She described the frequent fights between her parents as traumatic and a devastating secret.

"Little Viola had a whole technique of leaving my body," she said. "I'd go into the bathroom, and I'd stay there for the longest time. I would focus on one part of my body—usually my finger—and I'd shut everything down. After a certain amount of time, I would leave my body and go up to the ceiling, turn around, and look at myself . . . and I'd dream."

During these out-of-body trips, Viola imagined herself without her dark secrets so people would see her in a more positive light. Only as an adult did she realize how damaging "disconnecting" with reality was to her mental health.

"I believe that what connects us is not just the joy, not just the achievements, it's also the sadness, it's also the pain," she said. "But in order for me to share that, I have to unpack it."

While Viola has achieved so much professionally, she explained that success doesn't equate to emotional healing, which is why she wrote her book.

"You have to reconcile and own your story," she said. "I didn't. I cut it out like it was the fat on an awesome piece of filet mignon. You cut out the fat, and you re-create the story you want to tell. The problem with that is you shut out the dark, but you also shut out the light."

During her 2017 Academy Award acceptance speech, Viola thanked her parents for "bringing [her] into this world." When I watched her speech live, I thought it was dear. But after I read about what she'd endured as a child, I asked her *how* she was able to say that.

"Here's what I know about my life," she said. "What I learned from a very young age is radical love. Radical forgiveness. Radical transformation. What I was giving my parents was an opportunity to grow. They gave me that ingredient that could have either killed me or had me grow in a way that some people never experience their entire lives."

Viola now has a beautiful name for what she used to call shame: Warrior Fuel. I told her that phrase—that transformation—made me wonder if she had now found herself.

"Oh yeah! I have. Little Viola is celebrating," she said. "She's sitting right next to me, and she's happy that she's finally being embraced."

Well done, Warrior! When it comes to painful stuff in our lives that holds us back, as the saying goes, we have to face it to erase it.

"I like me. I like my story and all the bumps and

bruises. That's what makes me uniquely me."

—Michelle Obama

## LETTING LOVE IN

I think some of the most difficult jumps I've made in my life have involved romantic relationships. As I've said, for many years they were my "sidecar"—a nice add-on to my life, but definitely not the main event. And after my divorce and cancer, finding a partner was the last thing on my mind. I dated a bit, but nothing serious. Until I met Joel Schiffman, in the most unexpected way.

In 2013, I released a book called *Ten Years Later*, and a friend asked if I could give a talk at a Wall Street event and maybe stick around and sell some books. I agreed, but on the evening of the talk, I was exhausted and it was pouring rain. I *really* didn't want to go. But I couldn't let my friend down, so I dragged myself out the door.

When I arrived, I realized I must've been a last-minute fill-in or something, because the guys in the room were clearly not my crowd. Nothing against Wall Street, but *my* folks are just more . . . Junior League–ish. At the event, there were only about thirty people and everyone was staring at their phone, waiting for my spiel to be over. So was I! I was talking as fast as I could. The only person paying any attention to me was my friend, and she was mouthing, *I'm so sorry.* I just wanted to wrap things up and get the heck out of there.

But as promised, afterward I took a seat at the signing table and autographed copies of my book that a few attendees were buying—mostly for their moms and meemaws, I imagined. Nobody was buying it for themselves. Finally, at the end of the line, a guy approached the table, and he was cute!

I asked, "And who would you like me to sign it to?"

"How about me?" he said, with a twinkle in his eye. Well, that caught my attention. I looked at him and thought, *How about you, indeed!*

On my way home, my friend texted me, *I'm so sorry. That was the worst.* I wrote back, *Who's Joel?* She responded, *On it!* And as chance meetings sometimes go, Joel and I started dating shortly after that. I was in sort of a "Why not?" phase of my life. Why not casually date? Having a weekend companion felt right. So, when I met handsome Joel, I thought, *Why not give romance a go?* From the first time we had dinner, I just liked him. He was good company, he had an easy smile, and I felt like I could be myself—eat what I wanted, say what I wanted. And as we got to know each other better, Joel seemed happy to keep things light and weekend-y, too.

Before long, we started adding weekdays to our weekend dates, and a year later, things were going so well that we discussed moving in together. And that's when it hit me: *He doesn't know what I have planned.*

You see, ever since I'd told my friend that I wanted to be a mom, I was determined that nothing would get in the way of starting a family. But Joel didn't know that. How could he? I'd only said the words out loud to her. I needed to tell him, even if that meant my most cherished dream might end things between me and the guy I loved.

I remember our conversation like it was yesterday. It was just a typical weeknight—as far as Joel knew—and we were in my apartment, sitting around after dinner.

"I need to discuss something with you," I said. My voice was calm and even, but inside, my heart was racing. I was putting everything on the line.

"Okay," Joel said, giving me his full attention.

"It's a big one, so don't answer me today. I'm about to ask you something, but please don't answer," I said. "I want you to sit with it, I want you to let it marinate, I want you to take a week, take a month, it doesn't matter, but please don't answer."

He was probably thinking, *Where are we headed here?* My chest was pounding, because I knew that if he said no, it was a relationship-ender.

"I would like to explore adoption with you." I slowly exhaled.

Joel looked me in the eye and, without blinking, replied, "I don't need a minute, and the answer is yes."

I literally fell onto his chest and wept. I sobbed, my tears a huge release of relief and gratitude. It was one of the first times I said the word "adoption" out loud. A huge leap of faith!

This exchange was such foreign territory for me. I've always tried to make sure the people in my life get what they want, but this was finally me asking for what *I* wanted. For Joel to say yes to me at that moment, as if it were a given, was incredible. This was my dream, and now I had someone I loved to share it with.

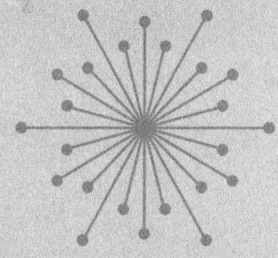

**"To love and be loved is to feel**

**the sun from both sides."**

—David Viscott

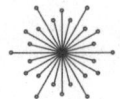

## MAKING SPACE FOR A LEAP OF FAITH

Once the decision was made to adopt, I could picture my life with a child. "Seeing" motherhood allowed me to believe it would happen. I visualized the connection like it was already happening! I used to sit at my kitchen table at night, and I could almost feel my baby near me. I used to say over and over, *I know that somewhere out there you are waiting for me, and I am waiting for you.* I just knew it was meant to be.

One day, after I was finally done filling out tons of paperwork, hosting home visits, and doing all the steps required to adopt, I just felt so *sure*. I was always certain about my decision to become a mom, but this day, something seemed different. Joel and I had recently moved into a new apartment that had one extra room, which would ideally serve as the nursery. That afternoon, Joel said, "You know what, I need some space, and they said it could be a year, so while we wait, how about I go ahead and use that extra room for my office?"

And I said, "No, honey, we can't do that."

He looked at me, a bit confused. "But . . . there's nothing in there."

"I know. But it has to remain empty."

"Okay . . . but why?"

"Because we have to make space. We have to make space for *her*. Because she's coming."

And I was right. In 2017, I was sitting in my office at 30 Rock doing a Zoom interview with *Today* nutritionist Joy Bauer when my phone buzzed. From the start, the adoption agency had advised me to pick up right away if they ever called, because time would be of the essence. When I glanced down at my phone, I saw that the "Ashley Project" (our secret code name) was reaching out. The text on my screen read: *Call me.*

My heart started racing. This was it! I interrupted my Zoom with Joy and told her I'd call her back. Quickly, I grabbed a yellow legal pad and wrote down the time: 11:53 a.m. This was the moment everything in my life was about to change. I took a deep breath and dialed the number.

Ashley from the adoption agency answered the phone and said these two words: "She's here."

My heart exploded! My daughter was here! I'd never witnessed a birth, but this was as close as I was going to get, and let me tell you, the feeling was amazing. That empty space we'd made for our baby was about to be filled with a lifetime of love and joy. Over the moon, I called Joel, my mom, my sister, my brother, and my best friends, shouting, "She's here! She's here! She's *really* here!" It was beyond glorious.

Everything after that was a whirlwind. We received pictures of our baby girl, hopped on a plane to Texas, signed the paperwork, and brought her home. On a Monday at 11:52, my life was one way, and by Tuesday, I had a family.

"Ask for what you want. Believe that you deserve it, and then allow Life to give it to you."

—Louise Hay

## Jumpstart

### THOMAS RHETT

Ever since I welcomed my two daughters, so many parents have shared their amazing adoption stories with me. One of those people is country music star Thomas Rhett. I've adored his music for so long, and I've probably listened to his song "Die a Happy Man" about a hundred times. (Maybe add another zero!) But what I love even more is everything about Thomas and his wife, Lauren—their marriage, the way they've navigated his career together, and their beautiful family of six. When I sat down with him in 2023, I knew that they'd always wanted children, but he shared with me the unexpected way his first daughter entered their lives.

"I don't think anyone's ready to be a parent until you are one," he began.

Thomas explained that as newlyweds, a marriage counselor had advised the pair not to be apart for long periods of time as they began their life together. So Lauren, who'd graduated from nursing school, joined Thomas on the road as he established himself in the music industry. Eventually, that first year of travel together turned into five.

"I think my wife, at that point, had felt a little bit passionless," he explained. "She'd felt that her passions had to be my passions, and so we had a year of conversations about 'What is your passion?'"

When Lauren expressed her desire to use the nursing skills

that she'd trained so hard for, Thomas was all in. It was her turn to shine. So, while he stayed home and worked, Lauren joined fellow Americans doing ministry work with children in Uganda. And that's when their lives changed forever.

"She sent me a picture of her holding this little girl, and in Uganda, they'd named her Blessing. She didn't have any parents and no siblings that we knew of," he said. "Lauren said to me, 'We have got to help find her family or find her a home.'"

And then, on the phone with Lauren—nearly eight thousand miles away—something nudged his heart to take a leap of faith.

"I don't remember even saying it; it just came out of my mouth. I said, 'We'll bring her home.' And my wife was like, 'Are you serious?'" he recalled. "I'd just never seen my wife glow the way she was glowing."

The couple had been trying to conceive prior to Lauren's work in Uganda, so by the time they adopted eighteen-month-old Willa Gray in 2017, Lauren was pregnant with a baby girl! Over the course of the next four years, she gave birth to three daughters—Ada James, Lennon Love, and Lillie Carolina.

When I shared with Thomas that my two daughters were starting to ask questions about their adoption, he said that he and Lauren were navigating the topic as well.

"Adoption is one of the most beautiful things in the world, and I don't think at the beginning of it you think, *In six years I'm going to have to start answering some really intense questions*," he said. "What age is the right age for the conversation? How do I preserve their wonderful innocence? We try to be as honest as we can without the confusion."

I'm so happy for Thomas and Lauren. And I completely understand how a leap of faith can make your heart reprioritize what matters most.

"If music was number one for the last eight years, music is now number three," he said. "I love it, and I want to be great at it, but if me being great at music makes my parenting and my husband role suffer, what's it worth when I'm fifty?"

Yep. Thomas sounds like a guy who'll die a very happy man.

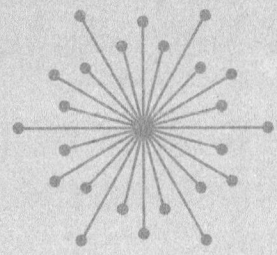

**"The purpose of our lives is to be happy."**

—The Dalai Lama

## Jumpstart

### MICHAEL TODD

As a pastor, Michael Todd fully embraces making family and faith a priority. He and his wife, Natalie, lead the Transformation Church in Tulsa, Oklahoma, and stay busy serving their congregation and raising their four children. But when I spoke to Michael in 2021, he told me that in recent years he's taken a leap of faith . . . in the opposite direction of his phone and the internet.

"If I could sum it up in one word, it's 'margin,'" he explained. "The greatest things I've ever done, they came in the margin. It didn't come when I was trying to figure it out or when I was trying to make it happen. It came when I made space."

As an example, in the quiet space where Michael chose to unplug—for a month—he came up with the idea for his first book, *Relationship Goals*, which became a number one *New York Times* bestseller. The next year, he leaped even farther away. He unplugged for one hundred days with a new baby and no fear of losing any professional or personal ground.

"Each one of us comes to this earth with a lane that we're supposed to run in, and it doesn't matter what anyone else is doing. What's for you is for you," he said. "When you don't stop to enjoy what has happened, to be able to look at all the amazing miracles that are your life, to enjoy the children that you work so hard for, you'll look up and not enjoy what you've built.

You'll get off the treadmill and be like, 'I've been running so hard to go nowhere.'"

Michael's a true believer that something happens in solitude that makes you more humble, and happier and healthier, too.

"Every time that I take this break or make space," he said, "what it does is it gives me the opportunity for me to recenter, for me to refocus, and for me to remember who I am, why I am, and who I'm created to help."

When I told him about my brief morning routine of journaling and meditating, he told me that he also creates daily "quiet time," reading scripture and writing down what's speaking to his heart.

"People aren't still enough or silent enough to even listen to themselves, to be able to see how they're feeling. And when I make that space every day, it's so crazy that one hour out of twenty-four hours can begin to set the trajectory for my life, my family, and for miracles that happen," he said. "In today's society, we let media, social media, our schedules, our children run things. We have not taken charge and prioritized the things that actually help us be healthy and whole and present in the moment."

Michael said that the sustained stretches of peace have revealed to him that he was trying to escape the insignificance and insecurity he felt as a child.

"What I was doing was running from pain and it came out looking like so much drive, but it actually was an unhealthy route," he said. "When I see people that are so driven and can't take a break and are proud to have vacation days they didn't use, it's a telltale sign that there may be something unhealthy in the past that they're actually trying to work and run their way out of."

Dang. I know it's hard to unplug—especially for long stretches of time. But Michael sure has some compelling reasons and results when it comes to taking a leap *away* from all the noise. Couldn't hurt to try. (And good for you, you're doing it right now!)

**"The quieter you become,**

**the more you can hear."**

—Ram Dass

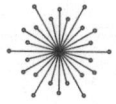

## HELPFUL TIPS AND TOOLS

Wheeeeeee! You've now decided to jump and are soaring through the air en route to your landing pad. Thrilling but a bit scary, right? Well, here are some of the "rocket boosters" I use to keep me moving forward when those pesky doubts come along for the ride. Maybe a few of these will spark ideas about what tools you can pack for your exciting journey to . . . (Fill in the blank!)

1. **I treat books I've already read—and loved—as a touchstone when I'm feeling a bit lost.** *The Book of Awakening* by Mark Nepo is one of my favorites. It includes bite-size nuggets of wisdom you can read each morning to set a positive tone for the day. I find that a good read offers another voice, which is helpful when the one in our head is driving us crazy. (If I need some title ideas, I'll search the go-to books of people I admire. What are *they* reading?)

2. **I've discovered the power of sixty minutes.** When my brain is spinning and my body is dragging, I'll shut myself down for an hour. I close the door to my office, turn off all my devices, and just sit quietly. I need to recharge! Sometimes it takes the entire time just to feel an ounce of peace,

but I never regret it. Carving out that time for yourself is the juice you need to keep pushing forward.

3. **Get curious.** As you move toward this new direction you've chosen, listen and learn. What can the people who've already arrived where you want to be teach you? I love to explore podcasts, TED talks, and commencement addresses for the motivation and information I need. Just search the curated lists of topics, for example, "Find me a TED talk about opening a bakery." So fun!

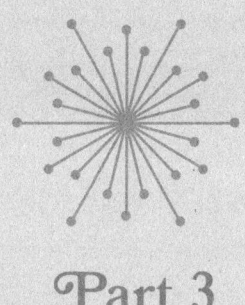

# Part 3

# Hop, Skip, and a Jump

Have you noticed it's the big, bold changes people make that tend to get all the glory? *Wow! Can you believe they had the guts to do that?* I get it. Those supersized leaps of faith in life are admirable, and when we make them—even more amazing! No doubt about it, major accomplishments get our blood pumping and our hearts thumping.

But I've also noticed that, while they're impressive, big wins often overshadow the little stepping stones that made our journey to greatness possible in the first place. (*Hello, we're over here . . . where we've been for years before your grand ta-da!*) That bold "big win" shadow is like a friend who barges into the middle of a group conversation and tells everyone to stop everything because *they* have an important announcement to make! All of a sudden, the story you were in the middle of telling—about deciding to get up half an hour earlier to write in your journal or exercise—seems small and silly compared to your friend's *major* news about making a career change, moving across the country, or climbing Machu Picchu.

But the truth is, we don't gain the confidence to make a big pivot without first taking all the little steps along the way to put ourselves in the proper position. Often, it's the little hops, skips, and jumps we make every day that have the biggest cumulative impact on our lives.

To me, these small hops are the unsung game changers in our pursuit of excellence. They refuel our tanks when we feel empty, make space for new ideas, and give us a sense of accomplishment. A little jump can offer a mini win, a pat on the back, a high five when we could really use one. Sometimes you only need a nudge—a tiny change—to chart a new course. Just ask the author of the inspirational book *Make Your Bed*, former navy SEAL, four-star admiral, and commander of US Special Operations Command William H. McRaven.

Admiral McRaven writes about the power of simple daily rituals like making his "rack"—the navy's term for bed—every morning. Not only was the task required of him, McRaven said it was the one constant he could count on every day.

"If you make your bed every morning," he explains, "you will have accomplished the first task of the day. It will give you a small sense of pride, and it will encourage you to do another task and another and another. By the end of the day, that one task completed will have turned into many tasks completed."

Now, you may be thinking, *Make my bed? That sounds like more of a chore than a hop.* Just one more thing to do in the morning when most of us are rushing around, trying to get out the door. Plus, we'll just come home and crawl into our bed anyway, right? Wrong, if you ask the admiral. I like the way he puts it.

"Making your bed will also reinforce the fact that little things in life matter," he says. "If you can't do the little things right, you will never do the big things right. And if by chance you have a miserable day, you will come home to a bed that is made—that you made—and a made bed gives you encouragement that tomorrow will be better. If you want to change the world, start off by making your bed."

A cool premise, right? And how exciting that simple little hops are all around us! Waiting for us. (*Hello, we're over here.*) What a relief to know that we don't always have to move mountains to move forward. Whether it's a bed, a conversation, or how we approach the day, the small changes we make in our lives *can* lead to very big—and meaningful—results.

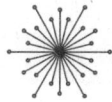

## TODAY'S THE DAY

Kids remind us all the time that their lives are full of firsts. I love watching toddlers point at things around them, spotting and acknowledging something they're seeing for the very first time. When you're a kid, every day brings a new task to learn or an obstacle to tackle. I see it with my girls all the time. I love watching them try something new and sharing in the joy it brings them when they *get it*. It's amazing! They're so proud.

And it doesn't have to be something extraordinary. Even a simple thing like saying goodbye to their little-kid Velcro sneakers and moving up to shoes with laces is a win. Remember how hard it was the first time you had to turn those two separate laces into one neat bow? Gosh, the whole thing seemed to take forever. But before long, it was no big deal. I think as we get older, we tend to dismiss the little victories and pass them off as unimportant when we shouldn't.

I remember spending a day with my daughters when Hope was five and Haley was seven. We had just gotten off the train heading back home from the beach and were still standing on the platform when another train came by. I looked over and saw that Hope had a little bit of her sneakers on the bumpy yellow safety barrier on the ground. Now, I wasn't worried; she was far away from the edge. But Haley, being the caring big sister that she is, said, "Hope, move back." She was being so responsible! That's when I decided it was time for me to take a little jump of my own.

I said, "Haley, today's the day." And she looked at me with her eyes wide.

"Today's the day?" she asked.

"Yup."

I had told my oldest that there would come a day when she could walk to the drugstore by herself. She'd been asking and asking for this tiny freedom, but I'd told her for weeks that it was too soon, that she was too young, that she wasn't ready. (Now I realize that maybe it was ME who wasn't quite ready for my little girl to start growing up.)

"Why now?" she asked me.

"Because you are careful," I answered.

And that's why I was letting go of a bit of control.

All the way home, Haley buzzed with excitement. The moment she'd been looking forward to—her first taste of independence—was finally here. I knew how much it meant to her, so the first thing we did was make a list. Now, honestly, I really didn't need anything urgent from the store, so I just made up a list of stuff that I knew we would need eventually— toothpaste, a shower cap, and cotton balls. Then I gave her twenty dollars and we put the list and the money in a Ziploc bag along with a note that said, *Hi! This is Haley's mom. Haley is allowed to walk back and forth to the drugstore by herself.*

I watched as Haley, clutching her little bag, marched off toward the drugstore. Her head was held high, her shoulders were back, and I could see how proud she was. Of course, I could tell that she was a little nervous, too. First times are like that. But I also knew she was ready.

As she got to the end of our street, she turned back to look at me, just kind of checking in. I nodded, gave her a big encouraging smile—*You've got this*—and held my breath as she continued her journey. This little jump was not just a win for Haley but also for me! I kept watching from the edge of our driveway while she walked the four blocks to the drugstore. The whole time, I was standing there, waiting, until finally, I saw her coming back with her bag of stuff. As soon as she was close enough, she ran and jumped into my arms. She'd done it!

I whispered in her ear, "This was a big day."

She hugged me tightly and whispered back, "This was the *biggest*."

My heart just about exploded with joy!

Opportunities for little firsts like Haley's are endless for children, but as adults, I think it's important to include ourselves in the fun of learning and growing, too. Maybe there's a little hop out there waiting for you to choose it. A "drugstore walk" that will make you feel as proud and excited as a little girl with her bag full of cotton balls.

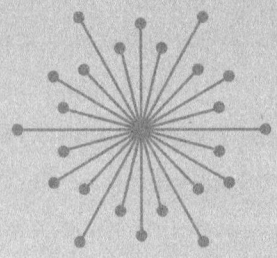

**"Jobs fill your pockets, but adventures fill your soul."**

—Jaime Lyn Beatty

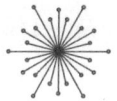

## SINK OR SWIM

It's *you* that has to be ready to take a little hop toward whatever it is you're considering. You decide what and when. Still, there are times when an unexpected someone or something may push you in that direction. I'm thinking of my mom, Sami, and how she learned to swim.

Now, I adore the water and always have. My siblings and I were fish from the start, learning to swim in the cozy confines of the Lakeview pool in Morgantown, West Virginia. In New York City, my daughters loved taking swimming lessons at an indoor pool just down the street from our apartment. But my mom wasn't so lucky—she had a much more sudden introduction to water, one she recounts with a mix of nostalgia and dread to this very day.

As she tells it: One day, as a child growing up in Egypt, she was enjoying a boat ride with her family. Little Sami was happily cruising along and soaking up sunshine. Then . . . *splash*! Suddenly, she became the ten-year-old face of the phrase "sink or swim." One minute, she was sitting on the boat; the next, she was thrown overboard! Her brothers thought it would be funny to push their sister out of her seat and into the water. But—no laughing matter—she didn't know how to swim! Talk about an unplanned hop, skip, and a jump. Now, many decades later, my mom loves the ocean and she'll spend hours by the pool. But she won't set foot on a boat.

The good news is, Sami did learn to swim that day. I guess sometimes we need a nudge (but please, not an ambush!) to learn something new.

"Sometimes in life, we all need a little nudge

to get us moving in the right direction.

If we ignore it, we're likely

to get a shove."

—Julie Ortolon

## Jumpstart

### BETHENNY FRANKEL

Chances are, you've watched Bethenny Frankel on television, read her books, or sipped on one of her beverage brands. The woman is an entrepreneurial powerhouse! A TV personality, businesswoman, philanthropist, author, and podcast host, Bethenny is a proven risk-taker. A self-proclaimed "Yes Girl." Bethenny's philosophy is to jump into opportunities and trust that she'll figure it all out as she goes along. One of her favorite sayings is, "Run with the big dogs or stay chained to the porch!"

To those who don't know her, the Skinnygirl Margarita mogul and BStrong disaster relief agency founder may seem to take one big jump after another. But Bethenny shared with me that it's important to be realistic and patient when you're first moving toward change. Her approach—and her advice to all of us—is to start small.

"Everybody needs insurance and a way to pay their bills. So have that, but you can still have your dream, too," she said. "When you get your paycheck, put ten percent aside and literally sock it away. And then spend an hour on your dream. Just keep going and see if you have time for both things. And then maybe one day, your dream will take off and overtake your day job."

I love what Bethenny is saying here. You can invest in more than one thing at the same time as you determine your next direction. Too often we think that the changes we make should be all or nothing. Go big or go home! But real life doesn't always work that way. Sometimes, we have to build our dreams on the side and as we slog through the day-to-day stuff that keeps us afloat.

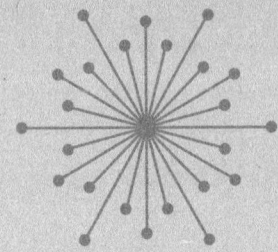

"Rome wasn't built in a day, but they were

laying bricks every hour. You don't have to build

everything you want today, just lay a brick."

—James Clear

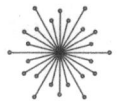

## SWEET SOUL

I'm always a sucker for something sweet. Whenever I fly, I bring along a giant chocolate bar to enjoy while I'm reading. I pop a small piece under my tongue and let it melt! I'm not saying it's a great habit, but I do love it. That's why it's no surprise that one day, when I lived in Manhattan, I connected with a young woman during an elevator ride in my apartment building. As the floors ticked by, I couldn't help but notice the beautifully decorated tray of cupcakes she was holding and the Oscar the Grouch hat she was wearing. I was totally into both. As I looked at Oscar's funny eyes atop her hat, I breathed in the heavenly smell of those cupcakes. Grinning, I told her my mouth was watering.

"They're salted caramel," she responded, beaming.

"Salted caramel! You can't beat that," I said as the elevator reached my floor and we parted ways.

Well, the next day, when I got home from work, the doorman stopped me. He said, "Oh, there's something here for you." He passed me two boxed cupcakes along with a little note.

*Hi, I was the girl with the Oscar the Grouch hat on, and you were admiring the cupcakes. They were all spoken for, but I had a little extra time, so I went to Brooklyn and I brought you these two.*

What? I couldn't believe it! That amazing girl took "a little extra time" and a little leap of faith that her tasty gift would get to the right place. Well, let me tell you, those salted caramel cupcakes *did* make it, but they didn't last very long. Delicious! What *has* lasted for many years is my memory of "Oscar," her sweet soul, and the power of small gestures.

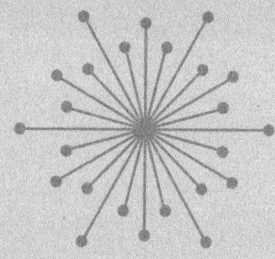

"In a world where you can be

anything, be kind."

—Clare Pooley

## FINALLY, YES

Usually nothing of great significance happens in a drugstore. (Except during Haley's big trip!) You grab Q-tips, a prescription, maybe a bubbly water, and you're out. No big deal. But, to my surprise, I had a very moving moment one day right beside my neighborhood drugstore.

In New York City, Duane Reade stores are on nearly every corner. They're the go-to place for drugstore stuff. So in 2017, I was walking there for baby supplies right after I'd brought Haley home. I was still being super private about the adoption, and outside my immediate circle of family and friends, I hadn't told anyone about it. I was just happily floating around in my baby bubble, elated, exhausted, and on this afternoon, in need of more baby formula. As I neared the Duane Reade, a woman stopped me. She had recognized me from *Today* and asked me if I had any kids.

Now, I had been asked this question loads of times before, and for years, my response was always the same: "No, but I have nieces, and I adore them." I'd said it so often that the words would just roll off my tongue. And I meant them! But now, standing there in the street, my usual answer got caught in my throat. "No, but . . ." was not true anymore. I stared at this sweet person who'd asked me a simple question. Was it time to share my news? Was I ready? From that moment on, my answer would forever be different.

I took a deep breath and—for the first time—answered, "Yes, I have a daughter."

Saying those five words to a total stranger felt like such a sweet little leap. I'd said it out loud! It was real for me and now for anyone else who asked. My goodness, I felt so blessed. I was finally a mom and could share that with the world.

**"A joy shared is a joy doubled."**

—Johann Wolfgang von Goethe

# Jumpstart

### PAT GARNER

I'm an optimist and have been my whole life. Thankfully, I inherited endless positive vibes from my mother, who believes that something good is always right around the corner. When I spoke to actress Jennifer Garner and her mother, Pat, on *Today*, I sensed that living sunny-side up is a choice Jen's mom makes, too, when she approaches each day.

During a commercial break, I was sitting with the pair on set and asked Pat about her flight to New York. Just some small talk. But her answers told me a lot about her.

"Well, I flew from West Virginia to Atlanta, and then the flight got canceled."

Savannah overheard and said, "Oh, the flight got canceled—what a bummer."

"Not really," Pat said.

"Not a bummer?" I asked.

"Not really. It wasn't so bad because here is how I look at everything in life. You can look at it one of two ways," she explained. "You can look at it like, 'Oh, it was raining, and I missed my flight,' or you can say, 'The plane didn't come in, and I missed it, and so what.' I just choose. Because either way, I'm not on the flight, and either way, I'm landing at midnight."

Bingo, Pat! I love that choice. To make little daily leaps of faith that everything—in the end—is going to work out as it should.

Her Zen-like outlook reminds me of a passenger I once noticed on a flight to Detroit, where I was headed to give a talk for NBC. My plane was sitting on the tarmac, and we were running late. And then *super* late. You know how it goes sometimes. When I knew there was no way I would make the speech in time, I called to let the event coordinator know. Kindly, she said, "Oh, we'll just have someone goose the crowd until you get here."

Forty minutes later, I was still waiting for the plane to take off. By now, everybody was ticked off about missing something and the contagious complaining began. One person started moaning about the fact that we weren't taking off, and pretty soon, everyone was grumbling. Everyone, that is, except for one guy. Wearing a suit with a briefcase near his feet, this man clearly had somewhere important he needed to be. Yet, he was an island of calm in a sea of angry people, just sitting in his seat, quietly reading a mystery novel.

I looked at him and thought, *There you go.* We all have two choices: get lathered up or sit back and relax. This guy had opted for number two. Just like Pat, he'd made a little leap of faith that everything was going to work out just fine.

**"One of our greatest freedoms**

**is how we react to things."**

—Charlie Mackesy

## Jumpstart

### SAM WORTHINGTON

Actors I've interviewed on *Today* are nearly always at the top of their game, starring in a new movie or directing an exciting project. They're the "it" celebrity of the moment, which almost always means they've taken lots of jumps—large and small—that have paid off, big-time. But then what?

When I spoke to *Avatar* and *Horizon* actor Sam Worthington, he talked about managing the constant highs and lows that come with working in the performing arts. An avid surfer, Sam compared navigating the ups and downs of his industry to riding a wave.

"You can talk to many actors, and they'll tell you at some point they'll be right on that crest, but then it's going to break," he explained. "I was told by Colin Farrell that it's up to you whether you get washed up on the shore or whether you want to paddle back out and find the wave of your choice."

I think what Sam was saying is that we have to trust that the waves will keep coming. Every day, we choose whether we're going to get out there on a wave again *or* let that particular one pass us by. Are we going to jump back into the surf (even when it feels scary), or are we going to sit this one out? There's no right or wrong answer. And your answer may be different from someone else's. The jumps you choose to make are your own.

"You learn to surf your way," Sam said.

I thought that was such a smart way to look at not only acting, but life, too! It's easy to convince ourselves that we have to stay up on the wave, stay at the top of our game, top of our class, top of everything! And yet, real life doesn't work like that. Sometimes, you're just paddling against the current . . . waiting. Sizing things up. I think "surfing your way" means learning how to pass on waves that aren't quite right for you. Taking a little leap of faith that there will always be another wave—*That's the one!*—rolling in. It might be small or it might be a monster. But it will always be exciting and new.

Feeling like it might be time for you to paddle out and check out the waves? Surf's up!

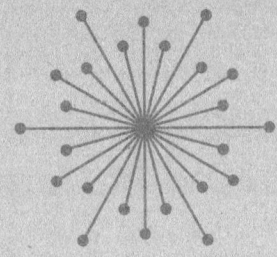

"Feelings are much like waves: we can't stop them from

coming, but we can choose which one to surf."

—Jonatan Mårtensson

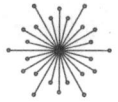

## TAKE A DEEP BREATH

There's no way around it. If you try to connect the act of breathing with jumping into something, it doesn't work. They don't go together. It's like when Jenna and I tasted a product for our "Yuck or Yum" segment that combined hot tamales with Cinnamon Toast Crunch. Yuck! Nope. They didn't go together either. But, I have to admit, when Jenna asked me to just *try* breathing in a new way, I was glad I took a little leap of faith.

The experience started with me setting up a Zoom session with an instructor named Christine whom Jenna had recommended. When we spoke, she directed me to place one hand on my heart and the other on my belly. She said to release all the air out of my lungs and then start breathing. The first half of the breath in focused on my lower body, the second half on my high chest. Then, I slowly exhaled through my mouth like I was blowing on a forkful of hot food. In and out. Got it. Seemed pretty similar to regular old breathing to me. I wasn't really sure what the big whoop was.

After a few minutes, I found myself getting nice and relaxed, and then I noticed something else starting to happen. I was getting emotional. Somehow this breathwork was triggering some feelings . . . and then my tear ducts. Suddenly, I exploded into sobs! I was crying so hard that I was practically hyperventilating. When I finally calmed myself, I asked Christine, "Um. What's happening here?" She told me that it was my body letting go of stress. Stress?

"What kind of stress?" I said. Christine asked me if that detail even mattered.

When I thought about it, the answer was, no, it didn't. Maybe all that pent-up stress had been caused by some big event, or maybe it was something small. Either way, I didn't want any part of it, and apparently, neither did my body! Afterward, I felt better and lighter. It was like a weight I didn't even know I was carrying had been lifted off me.

Now, years after that first session, I still love doing all kinds of different breathing techniques. Once you learn what works for you, you can do it anywhere and it's free. So, I guess breathing and jumping really *did* go together for me! I'll admit that, but I'm still a "yuck" on peppers in cinnamon cereal.

**"Breath is the bridge which connects life to consciousness,**

**which unites your body to your thoughts."**

—Thich Nhat Hanh

## Jumpstart

### MEL ROBBINS

I'm a big believer in creating simple habits that make my life run a little more smoothly. Every night, I lay out my clothes for the next day, pack my workout clothes in a bag, and leave a full bottle of water in my bathroom so I chug it first thing in the morning. I'm always on the lookout for small hacks like those that lead to big results! As motivational speaker and author Mel Robbins says, "Small things are not small at all. They are the most important things of all. And they add up."

Here, here! I love what Mel has discovered about improving our day-to-day routines. When I asked her about the most effective tips she's encountered, she offered a few adjustments we can make to our daily lives, from the moment we open our eyes to the time we close them.

"I think in life, we focus so much on the big problems and things out there that we forget that big changes come from focusing on getting just the little things right every single day," Mel said. "Make small changes for yourself. Set yourself up for success by starting and ending your day right."

Mel's suggestions are designed to feel doable and sustainable. Good habits are meant to go the distance, right? Here are a few she offers.

Keep your promise to yourself and get up when the alarm that *you set* rings.

High-five yourself in the bathroom mirror after brushing your teeth. (Connect the two habits!)
Take a ten-minute power walk or move your body in some other way.
And don't let the world in during any of these rituals.
Don't look at your phone!

When it comes to making it easier to reach your morning exercise goal, Mel suggests laying out your workout clothes so you don't have to root around for them in the dark. She also recommends setting a bottle of water next to your coffee maker so you remember to hydrate before you caffeinate.

Mel is a big fan of creating an evening routine at the end of your day that sets up the "tomorrow you" for success: clean up the kitchen, pack the lunches, move the clean laundry to the dryer. Clean your slate.

"You deserve to wake up in a powerful way. You deserve to structure your day in a way that supports you," she said. "Setting yourself up the night before is the secret to waking up and having a great morning, and when you have a great morning it's easier to have a great day."

Sounds smart! Let's try to set ourselves up for success in a few small ways from sunrise to sunset.

**"Excellence is not a singular act, but a habit.**

**You are what you repeatedly do."**

—Shaquille O'Neal

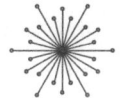

## FACE-TO-FACE

Daily life can be so busy that *any* extra time we have feels like a treasure. It's a gift! But when we consider how to use it, we may not think about something as simple as having a face-to-face conversation with someone we love. We're all so plugged in these days—staring into our phones, posting, and texting—that it's easy to forget the power of a good chat across the table. Eyeball-to-eyeball.

As you may know, Maria Shriver is one of my most cherished friends. She's my go-to person any time of day or night. I know that no matter what I'm going through, I can talk to her, and after just a few minutes, I'll feel better. When Maria and I chatted one day on my podcast, she dropped her usual wisdom bombs about life, including the importance of investing in friendship.

"I am conscious of the fact that I want to make sure, with the friends I do have," she said, "that I'm going deep."

I couldn't agree more! Her comment during that taping reminded me of a meaningful conversation that Maria, Jenna, and I had one morning. We were all in the makeup room at NBC, and Jenna had just flown in from somewhere. She'd been traveling for work a lot. She hadn't been home in days, hadn't tucked her kids into bed, hadn't stopped to catch her breath.

Hands down, Jenna is a hard worker—one of the hardest-working people I know. But on that day, all the running around was crushing her. She was exhausted. After Maria asked her where she'd been, Jenna started to tell her everywhere she'd visited and everything she'd been up to. Maria took a beat and then said, "Wow, that's a lot. Why are you doing all that?"

Jenna paused. She said that nobody had ever asked her that before.

Maria said to Jenna, "I just want to tell you something. And I hope you don't take offense to this. But I flew here yesterday, and the TSA guy said to me, 'Aren't you a Kennedy?' Jenna, I've worked my whole life to be Maria Shriver. But now I'm in my sixties, and they still think, *Aren't you a Kennedy?* So, I don't know what you're trying to prove, but make sure you're doing it because you love it and it fills you up. And not because you need to prove anything, because you don't."

Wow. That brief but deep conversation gave Jenna a lot to consider. A fresh perspective that may have lightened her load.

Hmm. That gives me an idea. Next time you're given a nugget of extra time, perhaps spend it talking with someone you care about . . . in person. Make a coffee date, do a walk-and-talk with an old friend—or with someone new. Who knows? A little leap of faith that spending time with someone will pay off in a meaningful way is intriguing. And it might just become a monthly routine!

"There is nothing better than a friend,

unless it is a friend with chocolate."

—Linda Grayson

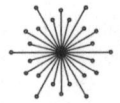

## SHARE THE LOAD

As busy as we are, the urge to "do it all" is real, especially for moms. We put so much pressure on ourselves at home and work—even when we're planning a family vacation! After all, carving out the time and saving the bucks for a great getaway can be challenging, so when we finally do, we want everything to be *perfect*! But inevitably, that high bar we've set comes crashing down onto our lovely little umbrella drink, and we're bummed. We've failed.

That's why a fed-up Boston mom developed a new strategy for trip-taking, and she shared it in an essay for *Today*. Amy McHugh said she was tired of taking charge of every aspect of the family getaway—an exciting destination, efficient travel details, and fun activities. She said that when her two daughters were young, the challenge was a little less daunting.

"But as they got older, the pressure to deliver a memorable trip felt monumental. Most of the time, regardless of effort, I failed to make both of my teen girls happy," she explained. "My unchecked disappointment often wrecked the vacation vibe—sometimes for a few hours, sometimes for an entire day."

It was during her divorce that Amy decided to take a little leap of faith and hand off the "good vacation" responsibilities to her college-age kids. She just sat back and put away her to-do list.

"My daughters took turns managing the trip details that have always spiked my anxiety," she said. "One snapped a picture of our parking section; the other redistributed items in our luggage in the TSA line. They led the way to our gate and pointed out my seat on the plane. Why hadn't I put them in charge years before?"

Of course, there were travel glitches and unexpected hiccups during the trip. But Amy said the whole experience was eye-opening in the best way.

"My daughters didn't care then or now if things were perfect. They just wanted to vacation with a mother who allowed herself to have fun," she said. "Truth be told, until this vacation, I'd believed vacations couldn't be enjoyable for me. I was a mom—do moms get to have fun on vacation? Now I know they do, if they prioritize their own experience as much as they do everyone else's."

Way to share the load, Amy! It'll be a while before my daughters can help me with our travel plans, but they sure are troopers when we go on fun adventures. Geez, all this girl-trip talk has me wanting to pull out my VACAY sweater and make some memories!

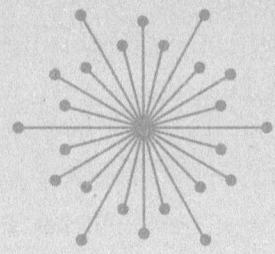

"One of the basic rules of the universe is that nothing is perfect. Perfection simply doesn't exist. Without imperfection, neither you nor I would exist."

—Stephen Hawking

## Jumpstart

### RACHEL PLATTEN

I can absolutely relate to anyone who considers themself a people pleaser. I *was* that person for many years. *Sure, I can do it* and *That's fine.* Ugh. Living that way can be exhausting, but sometimes we can't get ourselves to change. When I interviewed singer-songwriter Rachel Platten in 2024, I quickly realized that I was sitting across from a fellow reformed people pleaser.

"I was saying sorry all the time, explanation points after every sentence in a text, asking permission for everything, for my very existence," she said. "And out of that came so much rage. Why have I spent my life apologizing for who I am?"

Rachel said that along with a lifetime of burying her true emotions, she began to experience symptoms of postpartum depression and anxiety after giving birth to her daughter, Violet. She was having regular panic attacks as she struggled to cope with being a new mom and a touring artist at the same time. When she found herself sobbing on the floor of her studio, Rachel knew it was time to immerse herself in therapy, address her debilitating chronic pain, and experiment with a series of little jumps—new habits—to protect her mental and physical health.

"As much as my control-freak self wanted to think that I'm the one getting me into the rooms that I want to be in and convincing people, I just started to realize—what if I go with the flow a little more? What if I trust a little bit more and just do my best?" she said. "I'm going to be as honest as I can and as vulnerable as I can. And then whatever's going to happen will happen."

Rachel said this new approach left her feeling rejuvenated and empowered. So much so that she decided—at forty-three—to title her latest album *I Am Rachel Platten,* a proper introduction to the world.

Well, how nice to meet the rest—and very best- of you, Rachel. Way to battle for the person you want to be. (Is anyone else hearing "Fight Song" in their head?)

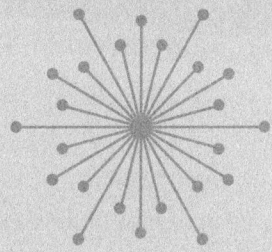

"When a woman finally learns that pleasing

the world is impossible, she becomes free to

learn how to please herself."

—Glennon Doyle

## Jumpstart

### OLIVIA MUNN

Life sure can wear us down, so any time we're able to remind someone that they're not alone in their struggles, it's a beautiful connection. That's what Aunt Harriet did for me during our "flash-off" in the bathroom when I was so self-conscious about my disfigured breast. Having experienced feeling alone and ashamed, I was so moved by the brave decision actress Olivia Munn made when she appeared in a Skims commercial during breast cancer awareness month.

A year and a half earlier, she had endured several surgeries—including a double mastectomy—after she was diagnosed with an aggressive form of breast cancer. She told *Today* that during the Skims photo shoot for shapewear and leggings, the scars on her breasts were not supposed to be seen. But when the makeup artist had trouble covering them up, Olivia took a little leap of faith.

"I was looking in the mirror, and I just thought, *I'm done being insecure about my scars*," she recalled. "So I went to the team at Skims, and I said, 'What do you guys think about showing my scars in this campaign?' And they were so amazing and thoughtful and wonderful. And we talked it out, and we decided to do it."

As author Kaitlyn Bouchillon writes, "Maybe, somehow, scars are actually miracles written on skin," and certainly Olivia would agree. She said she's proud of the photos and now views her scars as proof of how hard she—and so many others—has fought to survive the disease.

"Knowing there are so many women that have these same scars as me, I know that so many of them feel the same way I felt about them for so long. And I hope that they see the Skims campaign," she said. "Skims is so iconic and associated with beauty and sex appeal, and cancer really doesn't have that same connotation. So I just really hope that other women who have gone through my same path feel a little better after seeing it."

Lovely, Olivia! I know Aunt Harriet would be proud of you.

"I think scars are like battle wounds—beautiful, in a way. They show what you've been through and how strong you are for coming out of it."

—Demi Lovato

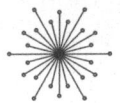

## FORWARD

There are times in life when we need a little something to keep us moving. To motivate and encourage us when we feel stuck or afraid. Personally, I love a meaningful quote or a positive affirmation, so it's not surprising that when I was dealing with breast cancer, I found the word "forward" very empowering. Keep moving. For years I wore a little pink silicone ring with FORWARD stamped on it. Turns out, that one simple word packed a punch for sisters Kristen Flynn and Sally Peterson, too. In October 2024, they joined Jenna and me to share their story of battling breast cancer just two years apart.

"Your world changes in an instant," older sister Kristen said of her diagnosis. She'd felt a lump in her right breast.

With no history of breast cancer in their family, the sisters were shocked to learn that Kristen would need to undergo chemotherapy, a mastectomy, and radiation. She explained that shortly after her diagnosis, a friend of hers attended an event where I was speaking, and that after hearing Kristen's story, I took off my FORWARD ring and gave it to her friend. At the time, I said, "Please give this to your friend Kristen for me, and tell her that I'm thinking of her and that she will be okay." As Kristen recounted her story and handed me my now-weathered little pink ring, I wiped away tears. Talk about a full-circle moment.

That simple ring had inspired Kristen's mom, Mimi, to order more just like it for her family and friends. "Everybody wore it as a symbol of moving forward," she said. It was their way of reminding themselves that Kristen would get through this challenging time. And she did.

But just two years later, Kristen's younger sister, Sally, got her own breast cancer diagnosis and needed the same treatment.

"It was shocking and devastating. I had three little boys at home, and I was so scared and worried about them, and I wanted to be there to take care of them," Sally recalled.

Kristen fully understood how scared her younger sister was. She also knew what Sally needed to hear: that she would be okay and her life would move *forward*. This time, Kristen ordered rings for everyone to wear in support.

Thankfully, both sisters are now healthy and happy, and their desire to keep moving ahead and living life to the fullest is stronger than ever. They even agreed to let us treat them to a style and beauty makeover on the show that day! And *wow*—these ladies looked fabulous!

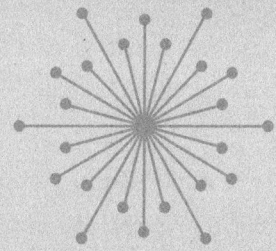

"Carry out a random act of kindness, with no expectation

of reward, safe in the knowledge that one day

someone might do the same for you."

—Princess Diana

# Jumpstart

## BRIANNA WIEST

As I mentioned, I love inspirational quotes. I've written two books in honor of those powerful little sayings! Well-crafted words can lift us up and make us think, especially when they come from someone as wise as bestselling author Brianna Wiest. I just love her book *The Pivot Year: 365 Days to Become the Person You Truly Want to Be*. In 2023, it was my go-to holiday gift, and people who received it fell in love with it, too. I ordered a ton, and when I was done giving them out, I reordered more!

I swear, no matter where you open Brianna's book, you'll find something that speaks to you. Her daily meditations have touched people around the world, inspiring them and giving them the courage to be the person they want to be. So, imagine my surprise when I interviewed her for my podcast and learned how much she'd struggled with confidence as a writer in college.

"I think I just assumed I wasn't smart enough or interesting enough," she said. "I was just kind of regular in a lot of ways. So I thought, *What could I possibly write or create that would be interesting to other people?*"

Unbelievable. This from a writer whose book I couldn't stop sharing with friends and colleagues! Brianna said everything changed when she began journaling to sort out her feelings and provide inspiration on her journey of self-discovery. Years later, when she looked back over her entries, she realized that what she'd written could serve as daily meditations to help nudge people to make positive changes in their life . . . over the course of 365 days.

"When I was putting the book together, I wrote it in that way because, over the years, so many people had reached out and said that something they really wanted and enjoyed was doing things a little piece at a time," she said. "An essay a day. Or they really enjoyed a post on Instagram. People are busy and they don't always have time to sit down and read a whole thing."

Brianna said that many of the daily devotionals she published were inspired by what bubbled up during her own ten-minute morning meditations.

"I think we think that our callings in life will come to us always like these huge clear visions. But I don't think they always come that way. Sometimes it's like a very small *Oh, I should go there or do that or create that thing*. Right? It starts tiny, so small."

Makes you wonder what your gut might be telling you right now, or why that voice in your head won't let up.

"So many of the things in that book," she said, "came from little nudges, little glimmers, little insights from that time."

Little jumps! I can't tell you how many people have told me that instead of doomscrolling on their phones before bed, they reach for Brianna's book to find inspiration and comfort . . . one page at a time.

**"Little by little, a little**

**becomes a lot."**

—Tanzanian proverb

## HELPFUL TIPS AND TOOLS

Even little hops and jumps require encouragement. Go, me! I love listening to music for so many reasons, but I'll always turn to it when I need a quick boost. After all, a song is only about three minutes long! Here are some of my favorites.

(How about making a playlist just for jumping? "Songs That Launch Me Higher.")

1. "So Will I"—Ben Platt
   I find this song so reassuring and uplifting. It reminds us that no matter what happens, the world *and* you are going to be just fine.

2. "May You Find a Light"—the Brilliance
   The music in this song is so ethereal and soothing, and the lyrics transport you to a place where you feel safe and grounded. You're home.

3. "Rainbow Connection"—Paul Williams and Kenneth Ascher
   What's more comforting than Kermit the Frog singing? His message is for dreamers and lovers and anyone with hope in their heart: wishes do come true when we believe in ourselves! (I love this song, too, because anything with rainbows reminds me of my Hopey.)

# Part 4

## Jump In with Both Feet

Sometimes, we only test the waters. *Dip.* Just one toe in. But I think over time, toe by toe, we may just find ourselves completely comfortable with two feet fully submerged in whatever challenge we've been tackling. The water's fine! Excited and proud, we may even be a little astonished. *How did I get here?*

When we accomplish something very meaningful, I feel like some sort of boundary has been broken. We've managed to finally scale a wall that's kept us trapped in the same place or state of mind. Perhaps we've relentlessly overperformed at work and landed a promotion. Or we've finally broken a destructive habit. Maybe we've healed an important relationship. Whatever the win, it's big and bold, and boy, was it hard getting there. All those little moments, decisions, and jumps along the way put us in a position to succeed. And while those around us may seem surprised by where we've landed—waaaay over there—our big leap has had to cover some major ground, with years and years of little launches along the way. As Pope Gregory I wrote, "You don't climb a mountain in leaps and bounds, but by taking it slowly." Ironic, right? We *inch* our way toward monumental change.

What I've learned in my own life is that you can't jump in with both feet until you've decided to start. To commit to something. The process of improving takes time, so the longer you wait to begin, the less time you have to experiment and learn and wander the messy path that is personal growth. You may wish that your big bold change is just a finger snap away, but it's not supposed to be. It's between the jump and the landing where all the good stuff happens.

So, when you're ready to start, make a plan that gives you a fighting chance to get to the other side of that big jump. Build your skill sets, find your mentors, maybe stash away some savings until all the pieces fall into place. Then, when it's time, walk up to that starting line like you mean it, pump your fist, and prepare to rock your world by leaps and bounds!

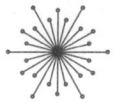

## FINDING MY SPARK

I'm not saying Bruce Springsteen wrote a song about me, but wow—a line in "Dancing in the Dark" absolutely nails the issue we faced when the fourth hour of *Today* launched. As you probably know, the Boss wrote the lyric "You can't start a fire without a spark," and was that guy ever right! In 2007, Ann Curry, Natalie Morales, and I were teamed up and told to "discuss stuff in the news." Easy, right? After all, we three talked for a living and were serious journalists. Ready, ladies? Cue the buzzy morning cross-talk!

Well, we tried. We were talking all right, but it turned out we weren't saying things that mattered to the people listening. Our conversations were a big yawn. With no experience as chatty talk show hosts, our vibe felt stiff and cold—and our viewers felt the chill. Everyone could tell that there wasn't a spark!

Then, one fateful day, when both Ann and Natalie were off, my producer Amy and I went to Michael's, a legendary restaurant frequented by media types, entertainment professionals, and power brokers. You never knew who you might see there, and the food was always delicious. That day, as we tucked into our meals, I looked across the room and noticed a beautiful woman. She was stunning and radiating star power. I was sure I recognized her from somewhere, but hmm, who was she?

Finally, Amy placed her—Kathie Lee Gifford, one half of the dynamic duo from *Live! with Regis and Kathie Lee*. A talk show legend!

"Hold on," Amy said, her brilliant mind working a million miles a minute. "We should have her cohost our show. It can't hurt, right? Let's go ask!"

So, we walked over and told Kathie that we loved her, that we missed seeing her on morning television, and, oh, was there any chance she'd like to guest-host an hour of *Today*?

Kathie had left her daytime gig eight years earlier and explained that she'd been busy appearing on Broadway, recording music, guest starring on television shows, and writing books. Even with all that underway, as cool as a cucumber and as nice as could be, she promised to check her schedule. Soon enough, we heard back and—thankfully—she said yes.

On November 14, 2007, Kathie Lee pulled a Springsteen and brought a much-needed spark to the fourth hour. She showed up to the *Today* set like a lit firecracker! Boobs out, hair extensions in, exploding with energy, and sharing amazing stories about her days with her kids and her former talk show cohost Regis Philbin. I was enamored. I'd never seen someone this hilarious and captivating in real life. Everyone else loved her, too, and it was easy to see why. Kathie's wild, but she's also a great communicator with a ton of on-air experience. She knows everybody, and when she freestyles? Look out. She'll break into song or find a vein of comedic gold and mine the crap out of it.

My first time hosting *Today*'s fourth hour with her just flew by. It was magic and red-hot! That set was fully engulfed. When the show wrapped, the powers that be from 30 Rock rushed over to congratulate her. They *never* came outside to the set, but that day they did. They wanted to tell Kathie Lee just how amazing she was, and she *really* was extraordinary. Her style—irreverent yet polished—had shown us all what the fourth hour could and should be. When Kathie was getting ready to leave, I called out—sort of kidding and sort of hopeful—"See you tomorrow!"

That groundbreaking visit from Kathie Lee was the result of multiple jumps. Amy and I jumped by asking her, and Kathie jumped when she said yes. She didn't need to do our show, but she did, and I could tell she loved it. I loved it, too. And the bosses upstairs, they *really* loved it. Not long after that, I started hearing rumblings that NBC was going to ask Kathie Lee to become a permanent host. Ann's schedule was already jam-packed—she was hosting four hours of *Today* while also covering stories all over the world—and Natalie was crazy-busy as a national correspondent and cohosting the nine o'clock hour. Their dance cards were full. As for me, I was saving a dance for Kathie Lee—*if* she'd have me.

To feel things out, she and I decided it would be a good idea to have lunch, just the two of us. We met at the Rainbow Room, a legendary landmark restaurant that's now an event space overlooking Manhattan from the sixty-fifth floor of 30 Rock. As we shared a meal and our personal journeys, day turned into night. The conversation was both deep and light, and we could feel a unique bond forming between us. We laughed and cried and sang! Well, Kathie Lee sang, serenading me with her incredible voice. I couldn't believe it! Our connection was instant and real, and we didn't want to leave. We closed the place down! As they were busy sweeping up around us, we said our goodbyes, amazed by what had transpired. Kathie looked at me and said, "I don't know if we'll be on a show together, but I know we'll be friends." I felt that way, too.

Days later, Kathie Lee went to my bosses and told them, "I'll do it, but I'm only going to do it with Hoda, nobody else." Incredible! I still can't believe that all happened, but I'm so grateful it did. I had no idea that my life was about to change by leaps and bounds.

When Kathie Lee took a seat next to me as my permanent partner, I'd only been a *Today* host for about seven months. I was a rookie! I'm sure the decision makers at NBC had more seasoned hosts in mind to sit next to the queen of daytime TV, but she had chosen me. And because she did, they did, too. Kathie took a leap of faith on me *and* on returning to daytime TV. She'd already found lightning in a bottle with Regis for many years. She didn't need to do it again, but she agreed to try.

Working with Kath was like watching a pole vaulter in action. She'd set her sights high and then launch herself with everything she had. I marveled at her bravery and her work ethic, too. Broadway, albums, books. She could do it all! But she was also the first person to tell you that there were more talented people than her out there. Kathie said that her approach was to maintain faith in herself and faith that she'd find a way to make her dreams happen. And she inspired others— like me—to believe in themselves, too. Who else could've convinced me to throw away my precious cue cards on national TV and just go with the flow? KLG did, and it made all the difference.

Looking back, I know now that *I* took a big jump, too. Transitioning from years of hard news to laughing and drinking on

TV with Kathie Lee was a huge leap. Until then, I'd reported from war zones and the middle of natural disasters. I traveled halfway around the world to cover breaking and often devastating news. It was scary saying goodbye to the one skill I'd honed for so long—being a serious journalist. Pairing me with Kathie Lee was a huge risk for all of us. I'm not the type of person who thinks, *Well, if it doesn't work, I'll just go back and do the thing that I was doing before.* That's not how I operate. I believe that sometimes, you just have to move forward and not look back.

That mindset makes me think of a story my friend told me about Moses. She said that people thought that the water parted when Moses walked up to the seas, but the reality was that he was submerged to his waist; he had to be immersed in the experience before the seas parted. Now, whether that fits your beliefs or not, I like the message. You can't expect a path to appear if you don't venture forward. You've got to get out there! I think there are times when you have to push yourself to jump in with both feet and say goodbye to what's behind you. You've come this far, so you're *probably* ready, and now it's time to commit, even when there aren't any guarantees you'll be successful.

I had to ask myself what I really stood to lose by taking this leap. And the answer was nothing. It was all gains! A new challenge, a dear friend, the opportunity to bring joy to someone's day. I realized that this new version of the fourth hour wasn't me reinventing myself entirely. It wasn't some lark. It made sense. I'd be utilizing all the skills I'd developed over the years, just in a new and exciting way.

Thankfully, my decision to jump over to the lighter side of

the news was validated when my workdays seemed like they were flowing. You know how when you're on the right path, things just seem to fall into place? That effortless feeling I had with Kath taught me that hard work doesn't have to drain you. *Good* hard work lifts you up and makes you feel alive. Like you're exactly where you're meant to be. On the other hand, when we try to force something that doesn't feel right, the hard work seems like a boulder weighing us down instead of a kite lifting us up toward the sky.

Together, Kathie Lee and I soared. We took a wild ride by each other's side for eleven wacky and wonderful years. It may not have looked like we were doing any heavy lifting on the show (unless you count those full glasses of wine!), but I think our chemistry and willingness to go with the flow lightened the load for a lot of people who tuned in to watch us. And, Kath, if you're reading this—cheers, my dear friend!

"Trust yourself. Create the kind of self that you will be happy to live with all your life. Make the most of yourself by fanning the tiny, inner sparks of possibility into flames of achievement."

—Golda Meir

# Jumpstart

## TIFFANY HAINESWORTH

I was more than twenty years into my career when I traded hard news for the KLG odyssey, so I'm always intrigued by how and why other people have managed to pivot later in life, too. Some of my favorite stories to watch were presented in a *Today* series we called "Second Acts." The folks we featured had embraced change wholeheartedly and transformed their work or personal lives by leaps and bounds!

Tiffany Hainesworth's story was especially compelling because her second act was not something she ever saw coming. She never saw the car that led to it, either.

In 2012, on the way to her job in Washington, DC, Tiffany was driving to get her morning coffee.

"I was getting ready to turn, and a car hit me from behind," she said. "He hit me so forcefully that it spun my car and he hit me again."

The second impact slammed Tiffany's head into the driver's-side window, and she sustained a traumatic brain injury. As a result, she spent five years in and out of the hospital managing her seizures and debilitating migraines. Tiffany had to be driven everywhere, and she also needed help taking care of her daughter.

"That was the most trying thing," she recalled, "because I had been independent for so long."

Eventually, Tiffany returned to work in government law

enforcement, but after thirty years in that role, she began searching for a more creative and rewarding job. Already making desserts and gummies with wines and spirits for fun, she decided to turn her hobby into a side business. She called it TCapri Gourmet Treats, a name that combined her first initial and her middle name.

"It was at that moment that I looked at how much money I was spending on other people's liquor," she explained.

Tiffany began to research what it would take to make her own tequila, her favorite boozy ingredient. In 2018, she flew to the Mexican city of Jalisco in search of a tequila broker and a distillery. She chose an area with higher altitudes and a colder climate where the agave plants produced a tequila with sweeter notes—exactly what she wanted.

"I was still having seizures, I was still sick, but I thought, *I'm either going to do this, or I'm not*," she said. "It's either going to work, or it's not."

To fully understand the process and to gain credibility with the farmers and the distillery she'd partnered with, Tiffany made frequent trips to Mexico. Using a Spanish-language translator app and her own muscle, she worked with farmers and learned how to harvest the agave. Five years later, by herself—no loans, no partners, no investors—Tiffany created her personal brand, TCapri Tequila. Little did she know that her leap of faith to change careers would land her well beyond her goal. Tiffany had become the first Black woman to solely own a tequila brand!

But that didn't mean that she stuck the landing right away.

Her brand launch in 2019 came with some significant challenges. Just as she began to grow her business, the pandemic hit. She lost correspondence with Mexico, and supply chain issues robbed her of the larger bottles she needed for her tequila. Scrambling, Tiffany bought the much smaller bottles that *were* available and created sample packs for customers. Finally, in 2021, she began personally delivering bottles of her tequila to local liquor stores, a proud and exciting moment. Three years later, TCapri Tequila was also distributed around the country.

"I actually went into this to have a couple of bottles of my own tequila for my gummy bears. That was all I wanted. Now, needless to say, I'm not making boozy bears anymore," she said. "I want people to see that although you've had adversities and trials and tribulations, you can still be super successful. But, you have to be focused. You have to be adamant."

Insert "strong arm" emoji here! (Maybe even two.) For anyone like Tiffany who's willing to go the distance—you got this!

**"All things are difficult before they are easy."**

—Thomas Fuller

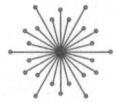

## FINDING TIME FOR TRANSFORMATION

As you may know by this point in the book, Maria Shriver is not only one of my best friends, she's my personal-growth guru. I admire the commitment she's made to learning in all ways and from many sources. Maria lives with an open mind and heart, and because of that, she's created so many meaningful experiences throughout her life. She's worked with the Dalai Lama, lived with nuns, and walked with Buddhist monk Thich Nhat Hanh. Imagine soaking up all that wisdom! So, when Maria once told me she'd had a life-changing experience that she'd trade her Georgetown degree for, I listened.

One night, we were out having dinner (early, of course!). Maria was telling me all about this amazing trip she'd made to California for a six-day retreat at a place called the Hoffman Institute, founded in 1967 by Bob Hoffman. She explained that the organization addresses the way we manage our thoughts and feelings and teaches participants how to go about rediscovering their authentic selves. Maria described the process as digging yourself up by the roots and replanting yourself. She called it "repotting" and said for her it was profoundly impactive. Geez. I could grow by leaps and bounds in just one week? Sign me up!

Now, I'd never done anything like this before, so I did a little digging of my own. Turned out, people from all walks of life had attended the Hoffman Institute. Some celebrities had gone, too—Katy Perry, Orlando Bloom, and Gwyneth Paltrow. The word that people kept using over and over was "transformational." Sounded promising!

Before I traveled to Hoffman, I was required to do some prep work. But honestly, no amount of paperwork could have possibly prepared me for what I was about to experience. My first thought when I got to the retreat was *Oh my God, what is this place?* It's kind of like a summer camp in the middle of the woods! It's beautiful and folksy and not like any retreat I've ever attended. Right away, everybody unplugged for the whole week. No internet or cell phones were allowed, a rule designed to help us tune out all the noise and tune in to ourselves. On day one, we gathered in a big open room. There were about thirty participants seated in folding chairs, and the leaders introduced us to the practitioners, each one proficient in the Hoffman process. Some of them were also trained therapists, psychologists, and life coaches, while others were artists, academics, or leaders in the corporate world.

When the facilitator asked participants to come up and say why they were there, each attendee began to share their reason. One person had lost their son, another had a horribly abusive father, and someone else was feeling stuck. As the moment approached for me to talk, I felt disoriented. It seemed like everything was moving in slow motion. My heart was pounding. I walked up to the front of the room and thought, *This is it—the moment of truth.*

I knew I could say that I wanted to better myself or something vague like that. But when I looked around at all the people who'd shared their raw truth, I felt so moved by their honesty. They deserved the same from me. So, I said it. I told the truth about why I had come.

"I am a total phony in my relationships," I said. "I'm a pretender."

Hearing myself say those words? I thought I was going to throw up. But at that very moment I had decided I was *not* going to pretend. I was going to be *real*. It was one of the best ten-second decisions of my life. From that point, I knew that I was all in.

The Hoffman process includes a whole bunch of different exercises and tools, like journaling, guided meditations, presentations, and play activities. Each day is different. One afternoon you could be doing exercises about awareness and another day the focus could be forgiveness. It's all part of what Hoffman calls the Cycle of Transformation. One of the goals is to help you find new ways of being, and let me tell you, after six days, I did! I felt like a completely different person. My baseline was different. The whole experience was—just as I'd been told it would be—*transformative*.

After the retreat, it's recommended that you take two days somewhere for yourself. A sort of buffer between Hoffman and reentry back into the world. I was reluctant at first, but I wanted to get the most out of the experience, so I booked myself into a hotel nearby in San Francisco. I arrived with all my notes and reading material and was struck by how in tune I was with everything. Six days of being unplugged and away from the pull of my cell phone and the internet had me looking up and around, not down and scrolling. I felt more connected with everything. I remember walking to the bay and seeing a group of women in the water. They were the only ones out there and they were splashing around. For a moment, I thought I should be ready to dial 911 or offer help. But then it became clear to me that they weren't in distress—they were delighted. I stared at them and yelled, "You all look fantastic!" They yelled back that the water was fantastic. They were laughing and high fiving. It was all so joyous that I was almost weepy! I think it's because I was seeing it so clearly for what it actually was and not what I had feared it to be. They told me to bring my bathing suit next time and join them! After that, I went to the pier, where I noticed a little boy fishing—all by himself. Normally, I would have been worried, rushed over, and asked him where his people were. But instead of reacting right away, I paused and observed. This kid was having a great time! I went to him.

I said, "You are a fisherman."

He looked at me and said, "Well, my sister is, but I'm not."

"Well, it sure looks like you know what you're doing," I answered.

He smiled and dropped his line in the water, and within one second a huge fish jumped on his line! He reeled that fish in with a big smile on his face. Next, his dad walked up and started congratulating him. I was applauding. We were all into it. And that little boy was so proud. He looked at me and said, "Usually my sister is the fisherman!" And then he released the fish back into the bay and dropped his line again. He was beaming. I mean, his whole body was glowing. The kid was pure magic.

I thought about how normally I would have been judgmental toward his dad, fishing all by himself while his kid was right over here. But that dad wasn't neglecting his kid; he was giving him space. He was in awe of his brave little boy.

Dad turned to me with tears in his eyes and said, "You're looking at the best thing I ever did with my life."

I could see he meant it. And if I had let my old Judge Judy self make assumptions, I would have missed this whole interaction. Instead, I got to share in their moment and learn from it. And that kid—he got another fish! I told him that this was the best day ever. He agreed and his dad scooped him up and spun him around. It was like a slow-motion movie, and I could've just walked by, been looking down at my phone or lost in my thoughts, and completely missed it. But instead, I was present. I was open and real, and because of that, I noticed things and saw all this beauty.

My life changed profoundly because of my time at the Hoffman Institute. Afterward, I could feel myself blooming and growing. I didn't feel the same as before, and I didn't have the same feelings about certain things in my life either. That included my relationship with Joel. Because I felt different, our "us" felt different. Everything had shifted. It wasn't like my new outlook happened overnight or in a week, but my time at Hoffman made it clear that I had been heading for a different path. And sometimes, when that happens, the love you have with someone transforms, too. It doesn't mean it's gone; it's just different from how it was before. And that's okay.

As we've all experienced in our lives, nothing stays the same. While the Greek philosopher Heraclitus said, "The only constant in life is change," the modern version might read, "The only constant in life is repotting."

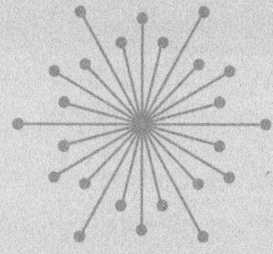

"In any given moment, we have two options: to step

forward into growth or step back into safety."

—Abraham Maslow

# Jumpstart

### YUNG PUEBLO

Ideally, we get wiser as we get older, so the tools we need to make impactful changes in life are in easy reach. And we know which ones to use for what "job." But when we're young, we haven't lived long enough to fill up our toolbox. We're empty-handed, so sometimes we stay the course, whether it's a good or bad one. We're still in the live-and-learn phase.

Thankfully, that wasn't the case for Diego Perez. His story of healing and change began in his early twenties, a remarkable turnaround for such a young man. His journey has inspired the millions who read his bestsellers and follow him on social media. Never heard of him? Well, you may know Diego by his pen name, Yung Pueblo, author of books like *The Way Forward* and *Lighter*. When I spoke with him in 2024, he described the challenges of being born into an impoverished immigrant family from Ecuador.

"As a little kid growing up in this poverty trap, I would see the stress of my parents. I would see the way they would argue with each other just to share their stress," he said. "My parents were still learning the language, so whenever we had a doctor's appointment, my brother and I would be the translators for the family, even though he was thirteen and I was eight. Sometimes, my brother would be on the phone pretending to be my dad so we could pay the electricity bill or whatever needed to happen. So, we grew up really fast."

Diego said he lived in an inner-city neighborhood in Boston where he watched his young friends join gangs, end up in jail, or—even worse—die. So, after tenth grade, he poured his heart into getting good grades and landed a scholarship to the prestigious Wesleyan University in Connecticut. Diego had jumped with both feet into a completely new life! But he wasn't equipped to handle such a drastic pendulum swing. No toolbox.

"All of a sudden, I was with the wealthiest kids in the United States," he said. "The combination of being in an environment that was totally different from what I grew up in and then having my own emotions coming up. That led me down this path where I was trying to medicate my emotions with drugs and alcohol."

Although many kids party in college, Diego said he was rarely sober and continued the substance abuse even after graduating. One night, at the age of twenty-three, he nearly died from a heart attack. He was so young! After that near-death experience, Diego knew he had to change again—but this time for the better. That's when Diego decided to finally stop ignoring his inner turmoil.

"I spent a two-and-a-half-hour period on the floor where I was trying to will myself into life. I felt like I was so on the edge," he recalled. "And in that moment, a few things really dawned on me. I knew I was wasting the opportunity that my parents gave me. That became really clear in my mind. I also knew that the reason that I ended up in this place was because I was lying to myself."

Diego said that on the floor, at rock bottom, he made the choice to change, to be radically honest with himself and break the harmful habits that led to this dark place. First, he stopped partying and started walking. He also chose to sit quietly with his pain, allowing himself to *feel* what he used to numb with drugs and alcohol. Next, he began to openly express the love he felt for his family and friends. Daily meditation also played a major role in his journey toward change.

"I think you have to remember that in the same way change can be difficult, it's also really beautiful. We have a very combative relationship with change, and we forget that all the things we love about life, the opportunities and the moments that have been created that have nourished us so deeply, they come from change," he said. "If this universe was totally static, nothing would exist."

More than a decade after tapping into the power of self-healing, Diego encourages people—and partners—to cheer on anyone who's taking steps to become more self-aware.

"I think if your partner really loves you and they're not interested, that's okay, but they should be supporting you," he said. "They should be supporting you and giving you the space for you to be the best version of yourself."

Wow, Diego. You've figured out all this stuff in half the time it took me! Way to go and thank you for sharing this best version of yourself with so many people around the world.

"We are products of our past,

but we don't have to be

prisoners of it."

—Rick Warren

# Jumpstart

## DR. WENDY SUZUKI

Trying to become more self-aware feels like a real workout for the mind—the brain! Dr. Wendy Suzuki, a world-renowned neuroscientist and dean of arts and sciences at New York University, is passionate about studying the brain and how it can drive growth and change.

"The human brain, *your* brain, is literally the most complex structure known to humankind. Think about that for a second. The one in our head right now. And it defines everything about us," she explained. "And so taking care of that is paramount in our lives. And that's what I realized early on when I decided to become a neuroscientist. And that's what I'm sharing with my students."

Wendy initially began her studies at UC Berkeley with a class called "The Brain and Its Potential," under the guidance of Marian Diamond, the first woman to receive a PhD in neuroanatomy from UCB. Before Dr. Diamond and her colleagues discovered brain plasticity in the 1960s, people believed that once we hit adulthood, the brain had developed and couldn't change. But Dr. Diamond wanted to test this theory, so she experimented with two sets of rats. The first lived in an environment without any stimulation. The other had a lot of toys and other rats to play with. It was like an amusement park for rodents! Both sets had free food and water. After three months, she learned that the outer covering of the brain, the neocortex, was thicker in the rats having fun at the theme park. Their brains *grew*. Her work proved that, in the right environment, our brains can change.

Years later, when Wendy was working around the clock to secure her tenure at NYU, she realized that *she* really needed an "amusement park." She noticed that she was tired and angry all the time. And the all-work-and-no-play routine had left her friendless. She knew she had to make a change. So, she jumped and booked a vacation—a rafting trip to Peru! During the getaway, she experienced the rewarding joy of adventure and making new friends. It was just what she needed, so she decided to keep the positive changes coming when she returned home.

"I started going to the gym. And I made more friends at the gym. And it changed my brain. I was feeling so good," she said. "I realized that it wasn't just that I was feeling good. People have noticed that sort of thing before. But my grant writing seemed to be better. Huh? What was going on? My memory seemed to be better. My focus seemed to be better."

Wendy realized that exercise was changing her brain, just like it had with the rats in Dr. Diamond's study. She then shifted her focus and created a class called "How Can Exercise Change Your Brain?" Wanting to bring exercise to her classroom but unable to get funding to hire a professional, she convinced the university to pay for *her* to qualify as an exercise teacher, and she began her experiment. Her students would exercise for a full hour before a ninety-minute lecture, but her colleague's class would not. Wendy would use the other class as a control group and test the brain and memory functions of each class, before and after, and compare them. On the first day of her experiment, Wendy greeted everyone in her best workout gear. She cranked the tunes and got her students moving. The class was doing Sati, which combines physical movements from kickboxing, dance, yoga, and martial arts and includes positive spoken affirmations.

"You have to yell things out loud like 'I am strong!' or 'I am inspired!'" she said. "And boy, there was a lot of nervous laughing in that classroom."

I'll bet there was! The good news is that the rest of us don't need to jump, punch, and shout affirmations for an hour to get similar results. Wendy reveals that we just need ten minutes of movement. Ten minutes to give our brains what Wendy calls a neurochemical bubble bath! That's a feel-good combination of dopamine, serotonin, and noradrenaline. Growth factors are released from our muscles, liver, and even fat cells. Every time we move, these growth factors go directly to the hippocampus of our brain. The part that's critical for memory and helps new brain cells grow. It won't cure or prevent Alzheimer's or dementia, but it can kick it down the road a little bit.

Unfortunately, Wendy was no stranger to degenerative brain diseases, as her father had been diagnosed with dementia. She knew she couldn't cure it, but she wondered if there was something she could do to change his situation while living with it.

"My realization was that as third-generation Japanese Americans, as adults, my parents and I never said the words 'I love you' to each other." Wendy wanted to change that. The question was, how?

"I decided that I was going to ask them about it on one of our regular Sunday phone calls. I decided that my theme was going to be keeping it light, like no big deal," she said. "This is a simple question. It's not going to be heavy because I wouldn't get through it."

Wendy's call with her mom started the same as always, with Wendy sharing details about her week. But before her mom could pass the phone to her dad, Wendy said, "Hey, Mom, you know, we never say 'I love you.' At the end of these calls, what do you think about the idea of starting to say that?" On the other end, there was silence as Wendy held her breath for what seemed like an hour. Finally, her mom responded.

"Oh, I think that's a great idea."

Waiting and wondering who would make the first move, Wendy took a deep breath and spoke in her best Disney voice. "I love you," she said. And her mom said it right back! Then it was time for her to catch up with her dad, and he also said "I love you" at the end of the call. When Wendy hung up, she said, she burst into tears.

"I realized that I had changed the culture of my family," she said, "and maybe changed the culture."

That's so powerful! The following week, Wendy's dad beat her to it by saying "I love you" right smack in the middle of their conversation. Wendy likes to say that her father beat Alzheimer's that day. He made a change in his brain by forming a new memory, one that she will always cherish.

And we'll cherish that one, too, Wendy! Thanks for giving us such powerful reasons to nurture *the most complex structure known to humankind.*

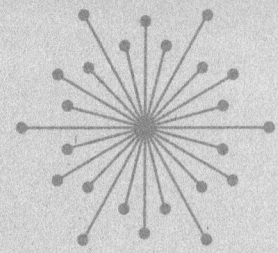

**"The secret of change is to focus all of your energy**

**not on fighting the old, but on building the new."**

*—Dan Millman*

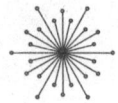

## THE PANDEMIC PUSH

Talk about learning to become more self-aware; the COVID-19 pandemic was a master class! After March 2020, a very unfamiliar "chaos of confinement" began to spread through our world like the SARS-CoV-2 virus itself. It was such an odd brand of chaos, too. It shook us up and slowed us down at the same time. Our lives and the world we lived in were changed by leaps and bounds. Forced to separate as a society, we were plucked out of our natural habitats and sidetracked from our daily routines. People dialed back their pace of life and became flies on the wall in their own homes.

The fresh view was, in many circumstances, eye-opening. *Wow! Is that what I do for a living? Really? I live with them? Look at all that stuff!* Lots of self-reflection happened during that challenging period, and as a result, schedules, relationships, and jobs were the focus of a revolutionary reevaluation.

According to a 2024 article published by our nation's census bureau, "an unprecedented number of US workers quit their jobs in the first full two years of the pandemic—a phenomenon dubbed the Great Resignation." All around the world, people were rethinking their work lives. The report defines what followed as the Great Reshuffling, with some workers leaving the labor market entirely and others changing employers. Boy, so much rethinking and reinvention occurred during that unsettling time. You probably have friends or family members who now do something completely different for work—maybe it's you! So many of us felt compelled to reimagine our professional and personal lives.

Yes, a pandemic is clearly a horrific way to produce tectonic shifts in society, but in 2020, one certainly did. Whether we like it or not, sometimes jumps are triggered by circumstances beyond our control and *kaboom!* We're unexpectedly airborne. Ideally, that's when we decide to spread our wings. When the courage to adapt and thrive sends us up, up, and away to an even better place.

**"When patterns are broken, new worlds emerge."**

—Tuli Kupferberg

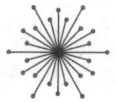

## LEAD WITH LOVE

Like so many other engaged couples, Joel and I put our wedding plans on hold during the pandemic. Ultimately, we split, but during our ten-year relationship, he and I made many meaningful jumps together. Hand in hand, we entered into a relationship, moved in together, got engaged, and adopted our girls. What a wonderful journey! But after a decade of being together, our next jump was to end our relationship while continuing our commitment as a family.

You probably know people who've experienced a similar transformation; maybe even you have. Ending a marriage but staying committed to making the kids a priority is not uncommon. I guess it just seemed strange to some folks that Joel and I skipped past the marriage and divorce part and went straight to the great friends and coparents part. But when you care about someone the way we care about each other, it's easy. We want the best for one another and our girls. Joel's a great guy, a great dad, and a great friend. Our decision to part wasn't one that we took lightly, but we knew it was the right one. It came from a place of love, not anger, which makes a big difference. There was no cheating, no scandal, no great big crisis. It sounds cliché, but the truth is, we were just growing apart. There wasn't the drama you hear about in all the great country songs. The no-good, two-timing, whiskey-loving heartbreakers. That simply wasn't us. (There are no songs written about real good, monogamous, coffee-loving coparents.)

Joel's a really nice person. I'm a really nice person. Sometimes, it's not that things are wrong, it's that they don't feel 100 percent right. I think when your partner is nice *and* there's chemistry, it's easy to overlook that you've been cruising along different paths. But when you decide to take a good look and compare road maps . . . you can't avoid the truth. Now, for some people, different is okay. Heck, some people get married but never live together! Whatever approach works for a couple is great. Everyone's situation is different. If I'm 100 percent honest, when it comes to romantic relationships, I think I still have leaps and bounds to go. I don't think I've ever really taken a deep dive into love. I've had loving relationships, but I don't think I've ever trusted that a person 100 percent has me, and that's on me. It's a vulnerable place to be and comes with the risk of being hurt. But it's a risk I want to feel comfortable enough to take one day. Which is why, after a few years of only going on playdates with my kids, I'm open to the idea of jumping back into the dating pool and going on adult dates with someone new.

Truthfully, I'm different now than I was before. I feel like I know which buckets I want someone to fill up. There's an emotional bucket, a fun bucket, a spiritual bucket. There are so many buckets in life! And when the time is right, it will happen. I really believe that. When I close my eyes, I can see it. I know it's coming for me. Not the version of me that someone thinks I am, not the former pretender or people pleaser who wants to make everyone else happy. But me, as I *really* am.

---

I think the key is to trust that life will give you what you want—and what you have worked toward—when the time is right. You need to have faith and believe that blessings are coming your way and that you are worthy of them. I think when you do that, your heart can rest easy. Mine is well on its way.

"I don't know that love changes.

People change.

Circumstances change."

—Nicholas Sparks

## Jumpstart

### SHERYL CROW

So many of us know what it feels like when the crapmobile rolls up and dumps not one but two steaming piles on our front lawn. It stinks! And I know the feeling. That's what happened when my marriage fell apart at the same time I was diagnosed with breast cancer. Not cool. You may recall that superstar singer, musician, and songwriter Sheryl Crow experienced *her* double whammy in 2006, when her relationship with cyclist Lance Armstrong ended and her breast cancer battle began. Talk about lousy. When I spoke to her in 2021, Sheryl told me that prior to facing cancer, her entire focus was work.

"I have measured myself for almost my whole life by my productivity. That's what gave me self-worth, and not just the quantity but the quality. It couldn't be ten songs, it had to be ten great songs, and they couldn't be ten top-two-hundred songs, they had to be ten top-ten songs," she explained. "But at a certain point, it's exhausting, and you wind up never feeling fulfilled."

But at age forty-four, when an annual mammogram revealed cancer, something a friend had shared with Sheryl years earlier finally resonated.

"He'd said to me, 'Everybody's intuitive. It's just whether you want to know the truth,'" she recalled. "And then he said, 'Emotions are the gateway to awakening.'"

Can we just stop here for a second? I love that so much!

*Emotions are the gateway to awakening.* Wow. We've got to feel to heal! Okay, back to Sheryl.

"I used to think, *Just stay busy. Don't dwell on it.* But that's the antithesis of what we need to do for healing," she said. "We need to actually sit with the pain, the anger, the grief. All of that goes along with getting to the other side. The only way to get through it is to plow through and experience it. And so, for me, I just embraced it."

Sheryl said she completely changed the way she managed her emotions. She didn't pick up her guitar. She didn't make a record. She didn't journal.

"And when I came out of it, I just felt like, *Oh, okay, I remember now who I am*," she said. "All of these events kind of help us remember who we are. We get so far away from it sometimes with all the messaging that we put on ourselves about who we are or who we aren't."

Not only did Sheryl rediscover herself, she realized that she could start a family—on her own—at age forty-five. In 2007, she adopted her son Wyatt, and three years later, her son Levi. Talk about jumping into parenting with both feet.

"Something really changed after the cancer episode and getting my kids. And if I never get to sing another song, I would still feel the joy that I feel right now. And that's a good place to be, for someone who always measured themselves by shucking and jiving through life."

I'm so happy for you, Sheryl, and I feel the same way about all the good stuff that happened to me after my one-two punch. Huh. Turns out those stinky piles are actually fertilizer that nourishes tons of personal growth!

"Right where you are is where you need to be. Don't fight it! Don't run away from it! Stand firm! Take a deep breath. And another. And another. Now, ask yourself: Why is this in my world? What do I need to see?"

—Iyanla Vanzant

# Jumpstart

## SIMONE BILES

I'm a Team USA Olympics superfan. (You may have noticed.) I love our athletes, and I adore gymnastics phenom Simone Biles. She's kind and funny and an ultra-fierce competitor. So, when she dropped out of the Tokyo Olympics in 2020, I was crushed for her. Imagine how hard that was! Simone showed immense courage by withdrawing from the sport she loves and dominates, knowing her decision would unleash an onslaught of both support and cynicism across the nation and the world. Most of us had never heard of the term that forced her to pull out—the "twisties," a dangerous condition when a gymnast's mind and body are out of sync. While some ill-informed critics labeled Simone a quitter, she knew her life depended on correcting the problem.

Intense psychological stress can disrupt an athlete's vital mind-body connection, and that was exactly what was happening to Simone. Pressure to perform at the highest level for years, trauma from sexual abuse by former Team USA doctor Larry Nassar, and constant scrutiny on social media had weighed heavily on her. But she had buried it all . . . until the twisties showed up. I think we can all relate to that—not making a change until our physical or mental health depends on it.

So for two years, Simone stepped away from training, focusing instead on her mental health. By 2024, when I spoke with her prior to the Paris Olympics, I told the twenty-seven-year-old that I felt like I was sitting across from a changed person. She agreed.

"I feel like the new me. I'm a little bit older, more mature, so just being unapologetically me," she said. "I feel a lot more free, especially going to therapy and doing those sessions so that physically and mentally I feel better. I know that's an important part of my routine, so just staying on top of that, it lightens the load a lot. I think before, I was kind of pushing down my trauma, and now I've learned to speak on it and kind of release that," she continued. "I think we used to think of therapy as a weakness, and now I think of it as a strength, and if there's somebody that can help me deal with what I'm going through, then that's what I need to do. Now it's a daily part of my routine."

Simone's hard work paid off exponentially. Her daily mental routine led to a series of outstanding physical routines at the Paris Olympics. (Where I screamed a lot.) She took home four medals, her second Olympic all-around title, a bedazzled GOAT necklace, and a renewed love for gymnastics—a real win for all of us who love to watch her perform.

We're so proud of you, Simone, and everyone on Team USA 2024! See you in Los Angeles!

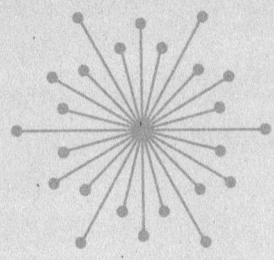

"Vulnerability sounds like truth and feels like

courage. Truth and courage aren't always

comfortable, but they're never weakness."

—Brené Brown

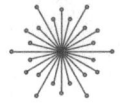

## GET GROWING

Clearly, I'll never be the GOAT when it comes to my guitar picking, but I knew that going in. Right before I turned fifty, I was determined to find a hobby. I wanted something fun and fresh I could tackle in my next decade! But, after I chose to learn how to play guitar, my initial efforts were hardly music to my ears. Wow—apologies to my neighbors. The whole experience was awkward and aggravating. My fingers felt like they were attached to someone else's hand, bent at odd angles with barely any strength. While my right hand strummed the strings—*down down up, up down up*—my left struggled to form chords on the frets. *What is happening?* I thought I'd never learn how to play an actual song.

Many of us struggle when we initially explore unknown territory, and whether we do it for fun or at work, I love what a guest on the third hour of *Today* said about that pesky learning curve. Dan Roth is the editor in chief of LinkedIn, so he talked about lifelong learning as it relates to our careers. While describing what skills employers find most attractive in a potential hire, Dan used a term coined by Carol Dweck, acclaimed academic and author of the bestselling book *Mindset*.

"The one that has been consistently rising to the top is this idea of a *growth mindset*," he said. "How do you approach a challenge? If you have an obstacle in your way, do you embrace that, do you constantly seek feedback, and if you fail, is that a learning experience?"

Dan suggested stockpiling as many new skills as we can and that we never stop yearning to learn. Even when the process feels clunky (and sounds horrible) at first.

"Computer languages, regular languages, leadership, negotiation skills," he said. "The important thing is to be learning and gaining new skills all the time because our jobs are changing quickly and if you only want to tread water and just do the job you have now, you've got to gain new skills."

I love the advice Dan offered to any of us who tend to beat ourselves up after we've taken a leap to learn something new. The vibe is like that wonderful phrase in the poem "Desiderata"—*Be gentle with yourself.*

"One of the key things you want to say to yourself," he said, "is 'yet.' 'I'm not good at this *yet.* I don't know how to do this *yet.* I'm going to learn in this opportunity.'"

During the time I was navigating my *yet,* a great guy named Jason Hagen helped me with my mission to become a six-string slinger. Or at least be able to play a song. With him as my instructor, I improved right away. After only two lessons, I started to nail the G chord and then E minor. The A chord followed. I was sounding better! Just four months after I started with Jason, he and I serenaded Kathie Lee and our guest Ricky Gervais live on the air with the song "Landslide." Talk about jumping in with both feet! I was so nervous, but I achieved my goal! As my skills got stronger, my hobby was even more fun, and I've stuck with it ever since. In 2022, Savannah and I went on Jimmy Fallon's show and strummed John Denver's song "Take Me Home, Country Roads." When Jimmy and the audience began singing along, I couldn't believe it! I wasn't even thinking *down down up* anymore, and I was belting out the lyrics, too.

That growth mindset sure did pay off for me. Eight years after I first picked up a guitar, I had improved by leaps and bounds!

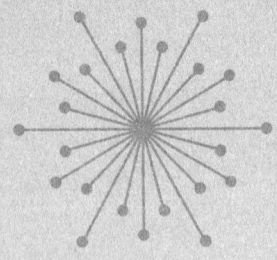

**"Every expert was once a beginner."**

—Rutherford B. Hayes

# Jumpstart

## YOLANDA TAYLOR

Saying "peace out" to a job you've held for years can be difficult. But leaving a career after three decades? Hmm . . . now what?

In 2024, *Today* featured a Maryland woman named Yolanda Taylor who said that from an early age, dressing with her own personal flair was a way to fit in.

"I was an awkward teen, and clothes, I felt like, turned me into a swan," she recalled. "I was really into it."

But as an adult, her love of travel led her to the airlines and she became an international flight attendant for Delta. During layovers in Paris, Milan, and London, Yolanda soaked up the fashion scene, still passionate about the industry. Her eye for styling clothes—even her work uniform—began to catch the eye of strangers and friends. So, in 2019, while still flying, Yolanda began a small business called At the Style Table.

"I'm not a hairstylist, I'm not a makeup artist, but what I can do is look at a woman and I see a beautiful canvas," she said, "and I just go to work."

But the same year she took on a side hustle, her father had a stroke and she became his primary caretaker. Then, the pandemic hit.

"I had to take care of my dad," she said, "and I had to be healthy, too."

So, after thirty-one years working in the air, Yolanda decided it was time for her to take a big, scary jump of her own. At fifty-three, Yolanda quit her job and began working full-time in the fashion industry.

"I was looking for my next life adventure," she said, "and this was the thing that I knew I could do and that I *loved* to do."

Now Yolanda helps clients of all ages purge their closets, update their wardrobes, and dress for photo shoots. Her favorite clientele are women in their later years.

"I understand women over forty, especially over fifty, who deal with issues from menopause. It's like a vortex from hell," she said. "Their body is changing, their emotions are changing, and when they look at themselves, they see themselves differently, and they can easily get into a style rut."

After decades in a different career, Yolanda said it's thrilling that her lifelong passion for fashion is now taking her sense of adventure to new heights.

"My high is watching women transform back to the women they once were," she said. "I'm going to be fifty-eight, and I'm all about how I leave this earth. I want to do something that makes a difference in someone's life, no matter what it is."

Talk about an inspiring *Now what?* The sky's the limit, y'all!

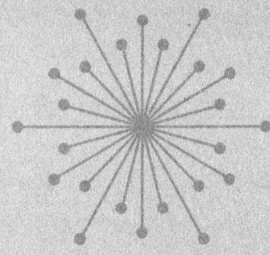

**"Let the beauty of what you love**

**be what you do."**

 —Rumi

# Jumpstart

## GABBY BERNSTEIN

Sometimes, the biggest jump we can make is to choose the hardest option. The one that seems entirely out of reach because we're flat on our back. When we've been knocked down in life or have hit rock bottom, the idea of making a change from that vulnerable position can seem impossible, let alone changing by leaps and bounds. I think that's why it's so important to see someone who *has* done it. Someone like Gabby Bernstein.

She's the host of the *Dear Gabby* podcast. She's also a spiritual teacher, a motivational speaker, a *New York Times* best-selling author, and a life coach committed to helping others turn their fear into faith. After facing her own struggles with alcoholism and addiction, Gabby reconnected with her spiritual life and transformed her trauma into strength, love, and freedom. Now Gabby has dedicated her life to guiding people as they heal from the past, feel worthy of greatness, and manifest a life beyond their wildest dreams.

In 2024, when I sat down with Gabby to discuss her latest book, *Self Help: This Is Your Chance to Change Your Life*, it just so happened to be the nineteenth anniversary of her sobriety. Listening to her journey, it was hard for me to imagine that the woman who's made an impact on millions of lives and written ten books had ever been a hard-partying public relations professional.

"I think about that girl in my studio apartment on the floor, on my knees, coming down from the drugs from the night before," she said. "I was so desperate. I said to myself, to God, to the universe—whoever was out there—I didn't know at the time. I said, 'If there's a higher power, tell me what to do. I need a miracle.' And I actually heard an inner voice. I heard a directive voice. And that voice said, 'Get clean, and you will live a life beyond your wildest dreams. Get clean.'"

That's when Gabby took a risk and embraced the hardest choice. How could an addict like her *possibly* get clean? Encouraged by a friend, she attended a meeting and found her sober community. Gabby said that she so badly wanted to feel better and be free of addiction that she stuck with her battle to recover. Finally, she was able to think clearly and pursue a vision she'd always had for herself: to be a self-help author and a motivational speaker. She slowly began to heal.

"There's this phrase that I was offered many times in my life: 'I wish you a slow recovery.' It's not the kind of thing where you just rip off the Band-Aid and you just dive right in. You can't just start to unearth all the parts of yourself that are so wounded and so traumatized because you will blow yourself out."

Throughout her years of "slow recovery," Gabby explored different methods and techniques to grow stronger. She discovered the power of Internal Family Systems therapy, which is based on the principle that our personality contains multiple "parts" that need space to speak, grieve, and heal. Gabby found it so helpful that she eventually trained in the method.

Today, she combines IFS with additional tools she's learned along the way to help and inspire others.

At the end of our interview, I asked Gabby, "Can you believe you're doing exactly what you always wanted to do?"

"Yes. I can believe it. That's what I love."

Isn't it such a relief when we finally believe in ourselves? Way to choose the hardest option and grow, Gabby!

"Always go with the choice that scares you

the most because that's the one

that is going to help you grow."

—Caroline Myss

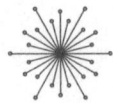

## HELPFUL TIPS AND TOOLS

Cue the party horns—you did it! You've jumped in with both feet . . . and made it to the other side. Feels great, right? If we accomplish something we've worked long and hard for, I think it's important to mark the moment. For me, celebrating is anything that simply makes me feel good. Here are some recent ways I've rewarded myself.

1. I flew to a sunny place to hang out with my friend for a few days, lie on the beach, and catch up. Great company, good food, and the ocean—what's better?

2. I got off my feet! On Seventy-Second Street in New York City, I sat in a La-Z-Boy for an hour getting a foot and leg massage. Amazing! By the time it was over, I'd fallen in love with the guy and his magic hands. "Let's just get married and start our life together right now."

3. I spent a while in the backyard swinging on my daughters' swing set. I felt so free! Something about the experience took me back to simpler times and I loved every relaxing minute of it.

# Part 5

## Jump for Joy

Don't you love when someone jumps for joy? Or even better, when *you* do it? Your soul is celebrating so intensely that your entire body is launched upward, over and over again. Arms in the air, feet off the ground, and you're screaming "Yeeeeessss!" at the top of your lungs!

Whew—joy is so powerful. I remember that deeply satisfying sensation when I held my daughter Haley for the first time. It was like heaven had created a perfect baby and dropped her right into my arms. As I held her tiny body next to mine, every cell in my being lit up and nothing else in that moment mattered. I'd waited so long to become a mom, and finally I was meeting my child. It was pure joy! Two years later, when Hope joined our family, I experienced that same soul-fueled celebration that blew my mind and filled my heart with so much love. I thought I was going to burst! My joy bucket was overflowing once again.

Such meaningful moments enrich our lives, and we welcome any and all flashes of happiness that come our way. I've found that making a big jump can often lead to the very joy we crave. When we get going, we get growing! And that makes us feel alive. It could be something impactful like becoming a parent, getting married, or landing the job of our dreams. But even small, simple pleasures can move us toward joy, like dancing as if nobody's watching or surprising someone with their favorite meal. Being joyful is always in reach!

And don't you find that it's contagious, too? If you see someone experiencing joy, you want to share in that moment . . . and then go create some of your own. But how? I think Arthur Brooks has a good recipe for living a happy, joyful life. As a bestselling author, acclaimed public speaker, and professor at the Harvard Business School, Brooks suggests developing a portfolio of four "habits" that become the foundation for lifelong joy: faith, family, friends, and work. He believes that when we nurture those four areas, we're investing in our happiness bank. We don't just *feel* happy, we're intentional about cultivating a happy life.

I sure love this concept. To me, it's empowering to designate four specific lanes to cherish, to work on every day. The areas that might just bring about that good ol' arms-in-the-air, feet-off-the-ground jump for joy. Wow! I can picture your hair bouncing up and down and your hands reaching for the sky as you celebrate an amazing moment. I hope you can, too!

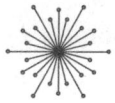

## ROOM TO GROW

The summer before I turned sixty, I was knee-deep in cardboard boxes. I had bought a new house and was packing up our pad in Manhattan. I'd been thinking about moving for a while, dreaming about what it would be like to give my girls more space—a home with a backyard, trees to climb, and a school they could walk to. I love New York City and always will. It's one of the greatest places in the world! But it's called the city that never sleeps for a reason. You can feel the energy, and the pace is fast. *Really* fast. The Big Apple had been awesome for me and my career, but it isn't what I grew up with. I remember walking to school, hanging out in my friends' basements, and riding my bike around until it got dark. My parents were strict, but I still had independence, and I wanted that for my girls, too. And so, we were headed to the 'burbs.

The little town we moved to is everything I dreamed of—just a train ride into the city but a world away. When I told my girls we were moving, I said, "We're repotting! We're going on a new adventure! New kids, new school, new everything!" It was a lot for all of us to take in. Big changes always are. Of course, the girls were nervous, but they were excited, too. Especially when I told them they'd each have their own bedroom! Like most families living in Manhattan, Haley and Hope had always shared a room. The same way that my dining room shared space with my living room and my living room shared space with my girls' playroom. It's just how big-city life works. But in the suburbs, I knew we'd have lots of room. We could put down roots and grow.

Our new house has been a perfect fit for the three of us and I knew it would be. I felt it the moment I first walked through the door. I could just tell that love had lived there and I was right. The previous owners also had two kids, one with special needs, and I could sense their goodness in every room. I'll never forget the first day the girls saw our new home. They ran through the house like it was Disney World! They went upstairs and saw their rooms, and they were jumping up and down and scream- ing with joy. Hope went straight to her jewelry box and started pulling out all her favorite pieces, putting them on like she wanted to get dressed up to mark the occasion. And Haley, she couldn't believe her new digs! She was splayed out on her bed and shrieking, "This is my room! *My* room!" I could see how much it meant to her to have a place to be herself, something we can all relate to. When they scurried down the stairs to the basement, the space must have looked like it was the size of a football field! Plenty of room to play and stretch their imagina- tions.

Our move to the suburbs was one of the best jumps we've ever made. Immediately, I saw a difference in my kids. They were running barefoot on the grass, climbing trees, collecting acorns, and swinging in the dark under the stars. Like I've said, I love NYC, but this was a whole other level of wow. Who knew that a patch of grass would be so important for my kids?

The neighborly vibe was amazing, too. We were welcomed with homemade pies, cookies, and many great meals. As we were getting settled during our first few months, we must've eaten across the street at our neighbor's house five times. They would say, "We're having pizza, come over!" or "We're throwing something on the barbecue, come over!" And over we went! Thanks, guys! I can honestly say that I went to more barbecues in those first few months than I had been to in my entire life. We even went to our first homecoming parade. There were tasty food trucks and all the kids marched around the school track. Haley even said, "That's my team!" We'd only lived there a short time and she already had a team! That night, it felt like the whole town was there to celebrate.

I remember taking it all in. New town, new neighbors, new experiences. Awesome. Moving is scary, change is scary, and there will always be hiccups, but that move put our roots down exactly where they were supposed to start growing.

Very quickly, I found out that my address change was an adjustment for everyone, beyond our little family. My friends and colleagues at NBC were teasing me and asking, "Who is this Hoda that went to the first day of school wearing sneakers and carrying her coffee in a thermal cup? What do you mean you joined the PTA and enjoy going to second-grade socials with your cool new mom friends? Hold up, did you say you were getting a *minivan*?!" I had to laugh. And yup! I did get a minivan. I needed it for carpooling. Carpooling! That was something else I'd never done before. Our list of "new stuff" kept growing by the day.

There's something wonderful about exposing yourself to new things, isn't there? Your heart's ability to expand is amazing; it just opens up and makes room for something fresh and different. Try it, and you may be surprised by how that newness can create a spark in other areas of your life. That one change—moving—led to so many other new experiences and friends and opportunities in my life. These days, instead of my girls jumping onto the subway to get to their after-school activities, they're jumping around in the backyard. Haley loves to spend time on the swings and Hope likes to tend to the herbs we planted, picking mint for my water as I breathe in the fresh air and read a book. I hear and see birds now and all kinds of woodland creatures, like bunnies and chipmunks. For twenty-six years I didn't have a close connection with nature or a neighborhood, and now that I do, it's a game changer. The start of a whole new chapter. One that I am just beginning to write.

"Joy is what happens to us when we allow ourselves

to recognize how good things really are."

—Marianne Williamson

# Jumpstart

## LAINEY WILSON

Talk about a down-home vibe—that's Grammy-nominated country music superstar Lainey Wilson through and through! The title of her fourth studio album, *Bell Bottom Country*, perfectly captures her cowgirl style and spirit. Lainey is such a gem that I chose to feature her on the milestone fiftieth episode of my podcast. As expected, she was warm and genuine, and I loved that jalapeño poppers and pajamas would be part of her day off *if* she could ever get one. It's her relatability—and powerhouse voice—that keeps her fan base loyal and her schedule jam-packed. Raised in a small Louisiana town, Lainey told me that listening to people in her community tell stories inspired her to write her own and set them to music.

"I was singing about tequila and cigarettes when I was ten years old," she joked.

By eleven, Lainey had learned to play the guitar, and she became a paid performer as early as eighth grade. Her parents cheered her on year after year, her normally pragmatic father encouraging Lainey to take a leap of faith from their small pond to big Music City.

"For some weird reason he said, 'Try,' " she recalled. "He was like, 'Yeah, this is it. This is what you're going to do.'"

At nineteen, Lainey moved to Nashville and lived in her camper. Starting over and making connections—both personally and professionally—flipped calendar pages and drained her resources. Lainey leaned on her parents now and then for support.

"They've had to help me at times. You can't do it without that, whether that just means somebody's guidance, or at times you say, 'I can't pay my water bill. Can you help me do that?' And they were there when I needed them."

After seven years of playing and praying, Lainey landed a publishing deal, followed by a record deal a year later. But still, the struggle continued.

"That meant I had twenty dollars in my bank account *with* a record deal," she explained. "My sister was Venmo-ing me for Taco Bell. I mean, that wasn't that long ago."

At ten years, one month, and a few days, Lainey would finally "make it" in Nashville, which is known as a ten-year town. (It can take a decade to catch a big break!) In August 2020, her song "Things a Man Oughta Know" went to number one on the Country Airplay chart, the first of many hit songs in her explosive career.

"I'm not going to lie to you," Lainey said. "I know a lot of people probably thought, *Man, when is she going to give this thing up?* But I never had that feeling."

Lainey's massive success in music led to an opportunity in a wildly popular television series. In 2024, she jumped into the unknown once again, acting in the hit series *Yellowstone*, a program that had already showcased some of her songs.

"I guess I've been scared to jump into things that I didn't know that I would be halfway decent at, even the acting thing," she said. "But it's crazy how the Lord blesses you with people like my parents. I have found people in Nashville and my manager, and at times they'll see things in me that maybe I don't see in myself. And they encourage me to take that step."

I'll always be inspired by Lainey's outlook on chasing dreams. Her instinct was to press on, that success was always right around the corner. And it was! Kinda makes you want to put on a pair of flashy bell-bottoms and go kick some tail, doesn't it?!

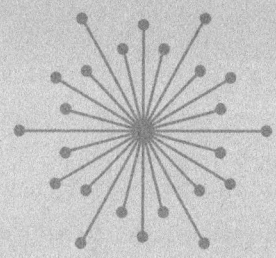

"I can't imagine a person becoming a success who

doesn't give this game of life everything he's got."


—Walter Cronkite

# Jumpstart

## ME!

Leaving home to pursue a dream—or for any reason—can leave you feeling funky and flustered for a while. I've certainly felt like a fish out of water plenty of times, flopping around and gasping for some sense of normalcy. When you move somewhere new, finding your pond and your people can take a while and it sure feels uncomfortable. But, after relocating a lot in my life, I've come up with a strategy to make any new place feel like home—faster.

Here's what I do. I fall in love! I make a friend, choose a favorite coffee shop, and find someone cute to date. I let myself fall in love with a new place and all it has to offer. Sure, some cities may never feel like your forever home, like Moline, Illinois, in the winter. But even there, I still found lots to love: my job at the news station, hanging out with my friend Chris Minor, and doing Maui Wowie shots after work at our favorite bar. So, don't worry if it takes some time to feel grounded following a big jump. Just keep your eyes peeled for all the good stuff wherever you've landed.

Look around and love what you see!

"If you look the right way, you can see

that the whole world is a garden."

—Frances Hodgson Burnett

# Jumpstart

## SAVANNAH GUTHRIE

A solid strategy that makes navigating anything a little easier is like a *Whew! I needed that!* During one of the busiest times in my life, Savannah Guthrie offered me a suggestion that had that same effect. *Whew!* My friend kindly recognized something I didn't even know I needed.

During our seven years together cohosting *Today*, Savannah and I not only worked side by side, we became close personally. Our kids played together and I got to hang with her family outside of work. What I've come to know is that Savannah not only has a big heart, she's able to see the people she cares about for who they are and gently offer a helpful suggestion if the time is right.

She did that for me when I was going through a particularly hectic time and was just plain worn out. You know how life can be go, go, go, with no breaks, and it feels like you're drowning? Well, I felt like that. I had just finished work on the show and was slumped in my chair, staring at my phone to see where I was needed next. Savannah came over and asked me how things were going. Going? Well, let me just check my insane calendar. But what she really meant was, how were things going for *me*.

Well, to be honest, I hadn't given *me* much thought. And apparently that was the problem. Savannah suggested, in that gentle way of hers, that I needed to add some *me time* to my calendar. It didn't have to be a lot, just a few hours once a week when our babysitter could be with the girls after school and I could do something for myself.

Hmm. A few hours to myself? At first, the thought of taking precious time away from my girls made me feel shameful. (*Hello, mom guilt.*) But when I thought more about my current frazzled state, I wondered, was I really doing my girls any favors coming home exhausted and grouchy? I knew the answer was no. Not only would I be better off having some time for myself, but I'd also be a better mother.

So I took a little leap and carved out time for myself during the week that I called "Thankful Thursdays." Instead of racing home after work, I went for a walk, browsed a bookstore, or tried something new that was good for me—breathwork classes, acupuncture, cold plunges. Then I'd grab an early dinner with a friend (I love a five o'clock early-bird special!), connect, and catch up. After that, I'd head home for a hot shower, some scribbling in my journal, and then a beautiful flop into bed. Instantly, I was hooked. Those special hours proved to be so effective at pumping up my mind, body, and spirit!

I loved the results of Savannah's suggestion so much that I continued Thankful Thursdays after I left *Today*. My girls know that Mommy loves being with them *and* that she needs a few hours to herself to be an even better mommy. Because I tried a new weekly routine, I no longer feel guilty about having time to myself, I feel *thankful*.

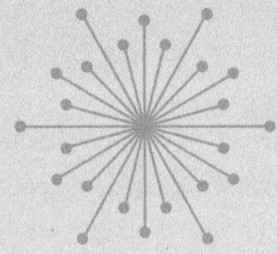

"Rest and self-care are so important. When you take time to replenish your spirit, it allows you to serve others from the overflow. You cannot serve from an empty vessel."

—Eleanor Brownn

## TURNING SIXTY AND TURNING THE PAGE

"Thankful" doesn't come close to what I was feeling in August 2024. A better word might be "astounded." If you'd told me when I joined *Dateline* that one day I'd be celebrating my six-tieth birthday on Rockefeller Plaza, I would've thought you were nuts. I wasn't sure I'd last even *one* year at NBC in those early days! I was so far out of my league it was like I was suited up in a different universe—that's how far out I was. I figured I couldn't be all that terrible because they'd hired me, but I was hanging on for dear life, begging correspondents to help me and show me how to improve. Back then, there's no way I would've believed that twenty-six years later, I'd be rocking out at work, surrounded by friends, fans, and special guests who had all gathered to mark my big six-oh.

On my actual birthday, three days before the plaza bash, I'd celebrated with my family at a delicious and fun barbecue. So, the party that NBC and *Today* threw for me wasn't just icing on the cake, it was like a giant cake on top of another cake! The hours-long festivities unfolded both inside the studio and out-side on the plaza, including a performance by young girls from the Harlem dance studio Groove with Me, a nonprofit I love so much. They played the song "Lil Boo Thang" by Paul Russell and soon hundreds of us were boogying to the beat along with those adorable kids!

But that wasn't all. To my complete surprise, the *Today* producers brought back three special families whom I'd met while hosting the show, whose struggles and triumphs had mirrored my own over the years.

- In studio that morning were NFL lineman Devon Still and his daughter Leah, who had survived the neuroblastoma she was diagnosed with at age four. Ten years later, I was thrilled to find that Leah was a lovely fourteen-year-old, healthy and thriving.
- I was also so happy to see Bart Conley, whose beautiful wife, Jill, had passed away at thirty-eight after a long, tough cancer battle. Her story was a reminder that not every cancer story has a happy ending, but there's honor and dignity in the fight. And that in the end, our love for one another endures.
- And I loved meeting back up with Frank and Stacy Parrado, to whom I'd had the honor of revealing that their dream of adoption was coming true with the arrival of their daughter, Addison.

Gosh, there we were. All of us together again after so many years. They had all touched my life as much as they said I'd touched theirs. Talk about emotional!

Throughout the party, I was crying happy tears and singing, too, thanks to power-packed performances by two of my favorite bands, Little Big Town and Sugarland. Minute by minute, people just kept wowing me, including an eighty-five-year-old mom and her four daughters who told me that they'd always wanted to meet me and had driven many miles to be a part of my birthday. Talk about humbling.

The whole experience was amazing, overwhelming, and way too big of a birthday party for just me, which is why I was delighted to see that the crowd included sixty women who were also turning sixty that year. As if it were a big, beautiful birthday card, a mural was revealed on a wall facing the plaza that was created by the Thrive Collective, a nonprofit whose mission is to create hope and opportunity in and around New York public schools. Creative kids in the program painted the colorful mural that features Haley's and Hope's little hands holding mine, and includes one of my favorite sayings, "Right on Time." The mural was one of two paintings I received that day featuring my girls and me. The other was from Jenna's dad, former president George W. Bush, and it hangs in a hallway at home that I walk through all the time. I love both works of art!

So many people went out of their way for me. I got a surprise video message from my pal and adoption inspiration Sandra Bullock, and an even bigger surprise when my dearest friends, Jane Lorenzini, Jennifer Miller, Karen Swensen, and Maria Shriver, showed up in the flesh! I couldn't believe it. Even my old college friends from Virginia Tech—plus the Highty-Tighties brass quintet and the HokieBird—turned out for a trip down memory lane.

As I stood there, soaking up all that love, I felt so grateful for everyone and everything, including this milestone birthday. For me, every single decade is like a clean slate, a chance to try new things. I'm not someone who looks back and thinks that my best days are behind me. After all, the greatest things in my life happened *after* I turned fifty. I got my dream job, and I became a mom—twice! Now, at sixty, I was celebrating with my favorite people and with those who were kind enough to join in the fun. The emotion that swept over me as I looked out into the crowd was complete awe. *It can't get any better than this.*

I knew I was riding the top of the wave for me professionally. This day was my very best at NBC and I could never top it. Looking back, I know I was experiencing what Maria said she felt when she was hosting large women's conferences as First Lady of California. People attended from all over the country and her events kept growing and growing. One day, Maria looked out at a packed room of attendees and thought, *That's it. This is the last one.* Everyone thought she was nuts, but she said she just knew the time was right. *It can't get any better than this.*

When I thought about what the next ten years might bring, change seemed to be on the horizon. My personal life was bookended by my aging mom and my growing daughters, and all three of them deserved more of my time pie. I wanted a bigger slice for myself, too, so I could love them and pursue new opportunities professionally. When I thought about the energy I'd need in this next exciting chapter, waking up at three a.m. five days a week wasn't the best recipe for feeling good. I imagined how awesome it would be if *I* could plan my daily schedule, free to prioritize who and what I wanted to nurture. To be honest, I was imagining a lot of what-ifs and why-nots leading up to turning sixty. *What if I gave myself permission to pivot? Why not imagine who I could be outside the walls of 30 Rock?*

But it was something Hope said that put words to my feelings. One day, she and I went out for a walk, and we came upon the tree she loved to climb. *Her* tree, as she likes to call it. She started her trip up the tree, grabbing its branches and hoisting her little body higher and higher. As she neared the top, she stopped and called down to me.

"Mom, what am I going to do when I get to the top of this tree?"

I smiled and said, "I don't know. What are you going to do?"

She thought for a moment, then looked me right in the eye and said, "I guess I'll find another tree."

And there it was. There was no denying what I knew deep down inside. I was ready to find myself another tree.

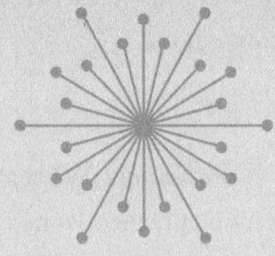

**"Don't ever live vicariously.**

**This is your life. Live."**

—Lavinia Spalding

# Jumpstart

### KAREN SWENSEN

I couldn't have made significant jumps in my life without the love and generosity of everyone around me. No one embodies both of those sentiments more than my dear friend Karen Swensen. She's always doing something thoughtful for others that doesn't cost much time or money. Years ago, while we were out having dinner, she noticed a group of veterans eating at the neighboring table. The next thing you know, she'd excused herself, talked to their waiter, and secretly paid the bill. I saw her do it, but she wouldn't take any credit when I asked her about it. She didn't lie—that's not her—she just brushed it off. Karen simply had faith that her small kindness might brighten someone else's day.

More recently, my amazing friend not only made a man's day; she also changed his life. On a blazing-hot Memorial Day, Karen was picking up a few things at her local Winn-Dixie in New Orleans. That's when she noticed a ninety-year-old man collecting shopping carts in the parking lot. She couldn't believe what she was seeing. A gentleman his age, working in such extreme weather—it was really concerning. A lot of people might have offered a worried glance or a sympathetic smile and kept going. Not Karen. She took a little leap, looked into his eyes, and said hello.

When Karen struck up a conversation with this man, she

learned that his name was Dillon McCormick and that he was a US Air Force veteran. He'd been working there for nearly twenty years, and he explained that this job wasn't just something to keep him busy in his retirement—it was essential to his survival. He told her that every day he walked more than a mile to work and back no matter the weather. And that was in addition to the several hours he spent in the scorching Louisiana sun, retrieving shopping carts and keeping the parking lot safe and tidy.

"He had the kindest smile and the greatest attitude," Karen wrote at the time. "Back and forth, back and forth, stacking cart after cart, sometimes more than twenty at a time." She looked on as he pushed and pulled his way through the maze of cars. "I watched a few others help him and thought the best way I might help would be to share his story." So she took another leap and set up a GoFundMe page for the veteran: "Mr. McCormick is working to EAT. He needs $2500/month to live and says he only gets $1100 from social security. So he must push carts in triple-digit heat to make ends meet."

As it turned out, other people were concerned, too. A lot of them. In just a few short days, Karen's little leap was amplified by the leaps of more than four thousand others who donated what they could to help. For Mr. McCormick, the result was life-changing. More than two hundred and twenty thousand dollars was raised! Karen was blown away by people's generosity, and Mr. McCormick thought the whole thing was nothing short of a miracle. Incredibly grateful, he said during an interview that if Karen was in the world, we were all in "good shape."

In November—nearly six months later—Mr. McCormick died from natural causes. How beautiful and meaningful that he and Karen crossed paths when they did. As she wrote on Instagram, "He died with dignity, knowing that the nation was truly grateful for his service. May he rest in peace."

"Never doubt that a small group of thoughtful,

committed citizens can change the world.

Indeed, it is the only thing that ever has."

—Margaret Mead

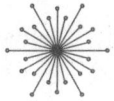

## BREAKING UP IS HARD TO DO

I often say that some days are just a Wednesday or a Friday—no biggie. But in 2024, a particular Monday would serve as the start of a whole new life for me.

September 23 began like any other weekday morning: I woke up at 3:30 a.m., showered, meditated, wrote in my journal, and headed to 30 Rock, my home away from home for the last twenty-six years. But what would come *next* was very different. My agent had flown in from Los Angeles, and he and I had a series of meetings scheduled. The time had come. This was the day I would tell my bosses and colleagues that I wasn't renewing my contract.

I remember feeling a crazy mix of emotions, my big news about to move from my heart to my lips. I knew the words I was about to share were unexpected, and that my decision would affect a wide range of coworkers and their plans. The list of people I needed to tell was long, and the order in which I told them was important to me. I was ending a relationship, the longest of my adult life, and breakups are hard. And breaking up over and over is unbearable. I felt like I had been cast in that Bill Murray movie *Groundhog Day*, where he's trapped in a time loop and forced to relive the same events again and again. You'd think it would have gotten easier each time, but believe me, it didn't.

The first person I reached out to was my boss and friend, Libby Leist, the executive vice president of *Today* and NBC News. I asked her to visit my office, where I was sitting quietly, my candles lit, Emilia Jones's cover of Joni Mitchell's song "Both Sides Now" playing in the background. When Libby walked in, she took one look at me and said, "Oh no." And I just started talking. I told her that I was thinking a lot about this time in my life and numbers and how I felt about the math. Twenty-six years at NBC News, with overlapping duties: ten years at *Dateline*, seven on the seven o'clock hour, sixteen on the ten o'clock hour. And I had just turned sixty.

Libby listened as I explained that I'd been asking myself what I wanted this next decade to look like. And that the answer was I wanted it to be different from my fifties. I wanted it to have more adventure, and I wanted to chase something, try something scary, go for something that didn't have a net. I said that my family formed in my fifties, and now my professional life would transform in my sixties. I told her that I knew I'd have more financial security if I stayed at NBC but that I had to think about my kids. When you wait so long for children— like I did—you don't want to miss your time with them. That's when Libby burst into tears. She said, "As your friend, I'm proud of you and so happy for you. As your colleague and boss, I'm kind of freaking out!"

We laughed and talked and cried together. She asked me if I was positive, and I told her I was. Even though my heart was pounding, and I knew it was a big deal, I'd slept well the night before. Sleeping well after a big decision has always been my litmus test to know if a jump is right. And the night before, I'd slept like a baby.

After my talk with Libby, I called Savannah. I had wanted to tell her in person, but she was traveling overseas for a wedding. I reached her by phone and then waited as she tried to find a private place to talk. When I was done sharing my news, she got very quiet. Then she said, "God, you've got balls." I laughed.

"You've got courage," she continued. "I'll mourn for me and our show later, but right now, I'm just marveling at this whole thing. You're leaving something that's like gold in your hands, not because you don't love it anymore, not because you're tired of it; you're just deciding. And that kind of leaving is really something to marvel at." Gosh. How about Savannah? She always knows exactly what to say.

Next up was Mazz, a.k.a. *Today* and NBC News executive producer Tom Mazzarelli. When Mazz saw Libby crying and asked what was wrong, she said to him, "We've lost our soul." Well, if I wasn't emotional enough before, look out. I cried as Mazz hugged me tightly and wished me well. It was the best reaction I could've hoped for.

Then it was time to tell my beloved cohost and partner, Jenna, and our wonderful boss and executive producer, Talia Parkinson Jones. We met in my office, and I waited to share the news until we were all seated on the couch. Then, I began. "I have to tell you something . . ." But, before I could get another word out, they both shouted, "No, no, no, no!" I kept trying to speak but they wouldn't let me, saying that word over and over. Finally, I managed to tell them that this would be my last contract. Jenna started crying, saying through tears, "I only did this because I'm with you. You chose me, and we chose us, and now it's us. This is our show." When Talia asked me to stay for just one more year, I told her I couldn't. That I wanted to be able to be there for my girls and do basic things like walk them to school. That's when Jenna jumped in to say she could make that work. She was *sure* if I stayed on, it could be arranged for me to walk them to school one time. One time! We laughed at that. I knew their reactions were coming from a place of such kindness and love. The three of us kept laughing and crying and hugging. Boy, were we a mess.

Later, Jenna told me that when she called her dad sobbing, he thought someone had died! When she explained that her tears were because I was leaving NBC, he reminded her of an earlier call she'd made to him when she was just starting at *Today*. At the time, her dad asked her if she could handle being my cohost. He said, "Look, Jenna, Hoda's the star of that show. *Hoda*. Are you going to be able to handle that?" Jenna laughed and replied, "Yes, Dad!" This time, she said his words of wisdom were different. "Jenna, you're going to be fine because now *you're* ready." I couldn't have agreed more. It was her turn, and she was *more* than ready.

My final call was to my longtime buddy Al. No surprise, Roker did something funny when I told him my news. He said, "Okay, bye," and hung up. He hung up on me! I thought, *Well, he sure got over that fast.* But about five minutes later, he called back. "I was just so shocked," he explained, "and I couldn't process what you were saying." Then he showered me with that one-of-a-kind Roker goodness. We shared a laugh over the whole interaction.

Later that week, we had a staff meeting with all three hundred of us who worked on the *Today* show and the waterworks flowed. Savannah kept saying the tears were just love. Love on display, she called it. I looked around at my NBC family that day and felt their love. It was powerful. It touched me to my core, and *still*, I knew I was making the right decision. Even if I was pulling a "Hodini," as Jenna joked. She liked to tease me about always leaving a party early. She even mentioned it at that staff meeting.

"One time, Hoda left a party with my purse. She left the party early. And she's doing it again! She's leaving before the shots. She's leaving before the party gets going, before the music." Guilty as charged, Jenna! "You go to a party, everybody's chatting, and all of a sudden, she's out the door! And I'm like, 'Wait—did you leave? Because you have my purse in your car.'" Tears turned into laughter at that one.

Gosh, what a day. I was drained physically and emotionally. As I left the building, a beloved greeter and gentleman I adore named C. J.—the unofficial mayor of 30 Rock for the last forty years—rushed up to me and said, "What? Come in here!" He pulled me in for the biggest hug! Of course C. J. had heard I was leaving. Nobody in the news business can keep a secret! But I didn't mind; it was the perfect send-off.

That night, as I was lying on the couch in our new house, snuggled up with my girls, I just kept thinking about how everything felt so right. When the kids wanted to know how my day was, I told them that their mama had done a brave thing at work today, but before I could go on, I realized the rest of my story would have to wait. Haley and Hope had breaking news of their own—there was a new episode of *PJ Masks* on TV that we *had* to watch together right away! Heck yeah, we did. *Sigh.* I was right where I needed to be.

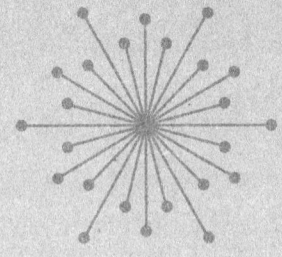

"Only I can change my life.

No one can do it for me."

—Carol Burnett

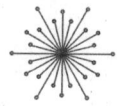

## WITH LOVE

This is the note I sent to my NBC family on the morning of September 23, 2024.

*To my* Today *family,*

*As I write this, my heart is all over the map. I know I'm making the right decision, but it's a painful one. And you all are the reason why. They say two things can be right at the same time, and I'm feeling that so deeply right now. I love you and it's time for me to leave the show.*

*My time at NBC has been the longest professional love affair of my life. But only because you've been beside me on this twenty-six-year adventure. Looking back, the math is nuts. Twenty-six years at NBC News—ten years at* Dateline, *seven on the seven o'clock hour, sixteen on the ten o'clock hour. I'm picturing your faces and your families and all the ways you've lifted me up and inspired me. That's my heart singing. So many of my professional relationships have become some of my most cherished friendships. Savannah: my rock. Jenna: my ride-or-die. Al: my longest friend at 30 Rock. Craig, Carson, Sheinelle, and Dylan: my family. Libby, Mazz, and Talia: my fearless leaders. I will miss each and every one of you at* Today *desperately.*

*I've been weighing this decision for quite a while—am I truly ready? But, my sixtieth birthday celebration on the plaza felt like a shift. Like a massive, joyful YES, you are! I saw it all so clearly: my broadcast career has been beyond meaningful, a new decade of my life lies ahead, and now my daughters and my mom need and deserve a bigger slice of my time pie. I will miss you all desperately, but I'm ready and excited.*

*Because I'll be working through the beginning of 2025, there's plenty of time to talk about what's ahead for all of us. But one thing I know for sure right now is this: everything's going to be just fine. The Peacock's feathers are never ruffled . . . no matter who comes or goes.* Today *and its amazing people—all of you—never waver. You always weather change with grace and guts.*

*Happily and gratefully, I plan to remain a part of the NBC family, the longest work relationship I've been lucky enough to hold close to my heart. I'll be around. How could I not? Family is family and you all will always be a part of mine.*

*Love,*

*Hoda*

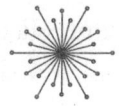

## MY NEXT BIG JUMP

"What's next?"

That was the question nearly everyone asked me when I announced I was leaving NBC. I guess most people know me well enough to assume that I wouldn't sit still for very long. It was a valid question, and one I'd been asking myself for quite a while. What *was* the next big thing? What was lighting me up? Turns out, the answer was a space I never imagined would fascinate me—wellness. But it had been growing on me for years. I'd incorporated breathwork and meditation into my daily routine, and I was a firm believer in the positive benefits of taking time out for self-care. I noticed how much better even ten minutes a day made me feel because those simple wellness practices had changed my baseline. I felt less stressed, more centered, and open. I was better equipped to deal with whatever life was throwing at me. The best part was that the tools I was using were easy to use, and they were affordable, too. What a compelling combo! I had dipped my toe into the wellness waters, waded in, and was now ready to dive headfirst into an ocean of possibilities.

I tracked down experts in the wellness field, read their books, listened to their podcasts, and invited them into conversations where I could soak up all their knowledge. Each new bit of information fueled my excitement. My wellness bucket was overflowing, and I couldn't wait to share what I'd learned with others. Not just my friends and colleagues, but the whole world! I wanted everybody to have access to such impactful information.

I started envisioning the different ways I could spread all this wellness wisdom. There would be weekend retreats where you could gather and grow. I imagined a mobile app where you could create a personalized plan based on your individual needs and personality. Affordable, accessible wellness right at your fingertips! *This* was my next mountain, my next "tree," and I was excited to climb it.

My first wellness retreat kicked off in October 2024 at the gorgeous Miraval Austin Resort and Spa, located on 220 acres of protected forest in Texas. It was magical and drew 150 people from all over the country. One woman told me she'd come to our event instead of a bachelorette party! A teacher told me, "I don't make any money, but we did get a bonus this year and I'm spending it on this."

I was so moved. I reassured them all that the difference between this weekend and a typical girls' getaway—or any weekend away—would be that the effects and benefits of a wellness retreat would last far beyond the event. I knew these women were taking a big step, investing their time and money in themselves, and I could tell that many of them needed to know that was okay. And it was. It always is.

I believe that everyone deserves a life outside of their work, family, and friends. Truth is, we can focus on those around us *and* make time for ourselves. Over the years, I've learned that if you want to be a fulfilled and vibrant person, you need to feel completed, not depleted. The key to being the best you can be is to fill up *your* cup first. After all, it's impossible to pour something out of an empty vessel, right? I know it's easy to think that denying yourself means you're giving your all to others, but in the end, you're just empty and run-down. And that's a lose-lose for everyone.

During that first event, the most important thing to me was that everybody could refuel *their* way. I told people that these two days were for them. If they were tired, sleep. If they came to reconnect with nature, go for a walk. Do whatever felt right—all of it or none of it. They had permission to define and design their own personal wellness journey for the next few days.

At the start of the retreat, before our activities began, I went for a sunrise walk with Maria Shriver. Soon, we happened upon a morning meditation where a group of Miraval guests had gathered. The session was about to begin and two seats were left, so Maria and I took them. We settled in, and what followed was one of the most incredible meditations I've ever had. Everything was so clear! I envisioned myself walking on a path, holding God's hand. I thought, *This path feels so right.* I looked behind me, and Haley and Hope were also holding God's hand. Then, they started to peel off and go in different directions. At first, I was a little nervous, but very quicky I knew everything was going to be okay. We were all on the right path. I felt it so deeply.

That meditation set up the whole weekend mindset for me. There we were, all of us on our path, coming together for different reasons. As an example, one woman had attended hoping that Maria could tell her what she should do. After Maria spoke, the woman approached her and described the challenges she was having in her professional and personal life. Over and over again, she kept saying that she was lost. But when she was finished, Maria gently explained that she didn't know her well enough to tell her what to do, but she did know that she wasn't lost. That instead, she was *seeking*. Now, swapping out one word for another may seem like such a small shift, but the difference was profound. The language and the way we describe ourselves matters. Maria had helped the woman redefine her situation. She wasn't where she wanted to be in her life, but she *was* taking a step forward by coming to the wellness weekend. She had started, and starting is the hardest part.

We were all seeking something that weekend, and there were a variety of events to help people find their way. The women participated in a broad range of activities and workshops, they enjoyed delicious meals, and they listened to live music. We also had an amazing lineup of guest speakers: Maria Shriver, of course, as well as author Arthur C. Brooks, professor Suzy Welch, corporate coach Manjit Devgun, scientist Dr. Wendy Suzuki, and entrepreneur Jamie Kern Lima, as well as wellness practitioners Anthony Abbagnano, Amy Rachelle, and Christine Goulding, who led breakout sessions. There was even a special performance by musician Rachel Platten, who performed eight songs that weekend instead of the three we were expecting (including her rousing anthem "Fight Song")! It was all so incredible.

One of my favorite experiences from that gathering happened during the breathwork workshop. For every exercise, strangers partnered up and stared into each other's eyes. The idea was to really see the person across from you and to let yourself be seen. It sounds easy enough, but dropping your guard and being so vulnerable—face-to-face—can be hard. In our last breathing exercise, we were instructed to focus on forgiveness. It was raw and powerful and some people burst into tears. Maybe they were forgiving others; maybe they were forgiving themselves. For me, knowing it was my last exercise, I thanked my partner and went to find my sister, Hala. I just felt like I had to be with her. It wasn't about forgiveness of anything in particular; I just needed to see her. When I did, we embraced and held on to each other as we cried. It was a release, like letting go of something we didn't even know we were carrying around. Afterward, I think many people felt that their load had been lightened, too.

That weekend, shifts and changes were happening all around me. You could see it in people. During her talk, Jamie Kern Lima told everyone to close their eyes and think about the part of themselves that hides in plain sight.

"Maybe you're afraid to speak up at a meeting because people won't take you seriously, or maybe you're afraid to put on a swimsuit because you don't like the way you look, or maybe you're an artistic person but don't think you're worthy, or maybe you want to be a writer but are afraid to put words on paper because you're afraid of what people will think about that," she said. "Now, picture yourself ten years in the future and think about all the things you will be missing about your life today."

Her words were a rallying cry for each of us to find the courage to let go of our fears and just *do the thing* (whatever "the thing" is in each of our own lives) rather than letting our lack of self-worth hold us back. Jamie spoke so beautifully about living authentically and embracing the true you. How sometimes your inner voice is quieter, and sometimes it's stronger. And that we can't hear our voice if we don't stop and listen. People seemed to welcome that gentle reminder.

When the retreat wrapped up, I looked at all the women who'd arrived on a Friday night as strangers. Now, after a transformative weekend of growth and sharing, they were saying goodbye on Sunday afternoon as lifelong friends. Everyone was hugging, and nobody wanted to leave! We embraced that magical feeling and lingered with it for as long as possible before we reluctantly headed back to our lives, forever changed.

Boy, witnessing the power of that weekend was so gratifying. My decision to spread the wellness word was a good one, and I could sense momentum building as I thought about my next steps. I realized that this was exactly what I was supposed to be doing. Wow! Those precious three days had crystalized what I'm most excited about pursuing moving forward: guiding people on how to be well by using accessible and affordable tools whenever and wherever they want. I feel so grateful and pumped and ready. As I write this, I can't wait to see where this big jump takes me—and you—as we stretch our minds and bodies in ways we never imagined. Let's *do* this wellness thing! Are you ready? Me too.

Right on time.

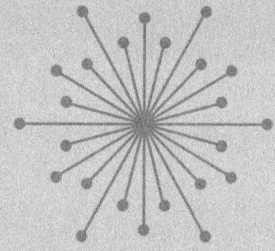

"And that is how change happens. One gesture.

One person. One moment at a time."

—Libba Bray

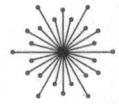

## THE DAY AFTER TODAY

Knowing that my work routine has been the same for decades, a lot of people asked me how I planned to spend my very first day after leaving NBC. One thing I knew for sure—I wouldn't be waking up at 3:30 a.m.! When I thought about how I'd spend the perfect Day One of my new life, I imagined this:

- Wake up around 6:30 and head downstairs to my cozy office
- Get settled in my office chair
- Light my candle
- Meditate
- Do breathwork
- Write in my journal
- Say a little prayer
- Get Haley and Hope up, dressed, and fed
- Walk the girls to school
- Come home and exercise
- a nice cup of coffee
- work in my office for a few hours
- for a walk
- Meet a neighbor for lunch at the local diner
- Enjoy a great conversation

- Head home for another hour of work
- Go pick up my girls from school!

To me, that seemed like the perfect way to kick off a brand-new (and joyous) routine!

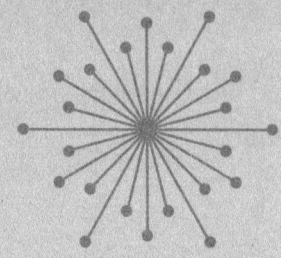

**"The key to knowing joy**

**is being easily pleased."**

—Mark Nepo

## WALKING THE WALK

Finally, I woke up to the morning I'd been dreaming about for years—my "Day One" Monday. On January 13, 2024, my eyes popped open at 4:15 a.m. *without* the prompt of a blaring alarm. I'd slept a big, beautiful extra hour, and it felt great. After a relaxing shower, I crept down to my office wearing cozy clothes and plopped into my office chair. I lit a candle and started scribbling, capturing my thoughts about this special day. Then I meditated for a while, clearing my mind and settling my soul. Around 5:45, I heard little feet padding into the room. It was Haley, in a T-shirt and undies, her bedhead hair fresh off the pillow. She whispered, "I can't believe you're here." We may have both felt like we were dreaming. She jumped in my lap, and holding hands, we looked out the window at a huge moon. I felt like she and I were in a movie, our faces bathed in silver moonbeams. We sat there, unhurried. Oh yes. That's my go-to word now—"unhurried."

Next, I helped Haley get dressed for school—a new routine for us both. When it was time to rouse sleepyhead Hope, she asked me, "Will you lay with me?" Of course I would! That morning was so cold that she didn't want to get out of bed, so we both giggled as I helped her get dressed under the comforter. All these weekday doings were so foreign to us that things got a little out of whack. There was some bickering at breakfast! After I got them fed and into their winter gear, I layered up, too, pulling on my *Hoda & Jenna* beanie hat. Filling my coffee mug was the final step.

At 8:00 a.m., it was time for me to stop talking the talk and start walking the walk . . . with my girls. After sharing for weeks that this simple rite of passage was a driving force in my decision to jump, I was about to actually do it. Smiling from ear to ear, I held my daughters' hands, and we started down the driveway to the street. Soon, we met up with other school-bound kids and their moms, a chatty little caravan. Some of the children grouped together, but on this day, Haley and Hope stuck with me. (We'll see how long that lasts.) When we got close to our destination, Hope asked, "Mom, do you want to walk me all the way, or do you want to see how I look when I walk the rest of the way by myself?" Of course, I chose to watch her. My big girl. Hopey made her way down the sidewalk and turned around to wave to me, her backpack swinging sideways. Haley was ahead of Hope, and I about busted watching Big Sis skip toward the door. I shouted, "I love you!" and watched until they both disappeared. Wow. I was so moved by the whole experience—those mere fifteen minutes—that I just kept walking. I needed time to soak up the moment and the memory. *Unhurried.*

Back home, I did a 9:15 spin class, showered, and had a few meetings—ordinary stuff. But all this ordinary felt quite extraordinary. For so long, I'd been living on either side of things, missing all that unfolded in between. Now I was present for every meaningful moment that fills up a day. Especially this one, the day I walked the walk.

"Enjoy the little things in life, for one day you'll

look back and realize they were big things."

—Kurt Vonnegut

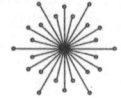

## HELPFUL TIPS AND TOOLS

What's better than pure joy? Maybe love, but both are the bomb—what we wish for ourselves and others. Heck, I chose Joy for Haley's middle name. It's such a powerful word bursting with happiness and satisfaction. To me, one of the best things about joy is how contagious it is. We feel it, share it, and pass it on!

1. One afternoon, my dear friend and driver Eddie and I were headed to a Broadway show. Traffic was backed up and we were barely moving. That's when Eddie decided to play the song "New York, New York." And he cranked that thing! Frank Sinatra was crooning, the city was bustling, and Eddie and I were totally into it. Suddenly, in a burst of joy, I found myself hanging out the car window, screaming the lyrics at the top of my lungs. Eddie popped up through the sunroof and started belting out the song, too. It was nuts! Then Joy did her thing and everyone around us started to sing along—New Yorkers, tourists, Who Dats. We were all feeling it together! And I'll never forget it.

2. For some reason, a black cloud was hanging over the makeup room when I walked in one day. Everyone was in a funk. "Nope," I said. "Not today." I cranked up my most

energetic playlist and turned that place into a dance party! Just like that, Collective Joy kicked Grumpy to the curb.

3. It never fails. Kids are the best at showing us what pure joy looks like. The other day, Haley was running around the house buck naked slapping her own tush and dancing to the Ed Sheeran song "Shivers." What in the world? I laughed so hard! To me, it's always a gift to share in someone else's pure, unadulterated joy. (Like Haley Joy's!)

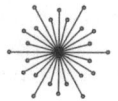

# Conclusion

ERE WE ARE, nearly three hundred pages later, and I'm wondering how you're doing. What you're feeling. I hope if you've been considering a change, the idea of it now seems a bit more clear or compelling. If you're well on your way to reimagining your life, perhaps something or someone you've read about in this book has added fuel to your fire. I think it's so important to know that people all around us have landed where we want to be, and that we can learn from their determination. As author Jon Acuff offers, "Be brave enough to be bad at something new."

As I write this, I'm three months into my big jump and it's been exciting and interesting and full of little adjustments as I navigate "being bad at something new." Right off the bat, I screwed up the breakfast rhythm that was working just fine for my kids while I was still working at NBC. By deciding to add music and singing to our eating-brushing-dressing-exiting routine, I blew up that finite window of time we had to execute it all. Big mistake. So now, I still blast music every morning, but we do our sing-along to Forrest Frank's "Good Day" on the way to school.

For some reason, I didn't anticipate how much I'd miss having daily interactions with people. I'm such a connections person, and for decades, connection came to me just because I walked through the doors of 30 Rock. Now, creating community is up to me. So, during the week, I'll schedule several coffee and lunch dates with neighbors and friends, one-on-one. It's always fun, and I'm reminded—every time—that talking with anyone who's been through something different from you makes for very cool conversations.

Adjusting to my new pace of life is still a work in progress. I sleep until 5 a.m. now! And even though my schedule is mine to create, every hour seems to fill up fast. I know I said my goal is to live "unhurried," but my jam-packed calendar isn't listening. Gah! I guess it'll take me a minute to figure out the right balance between slowing down and staying engaged with adventure.

I do feel healthier and recharged. Looking back, I realize how little sleep I was getting and how impactful it is to rest. For the first time in forever, I can work out regularly instead of cramming in exercise plus eating crap food on the go. (I cook eggs for myself every morning now.) I also feel a lot calmer and I can tell my kids do, too. Since they see me often, they're less clingy and more independent. It used to be that when I got home, they were all over me. I could barely move! But now, Mommy's always close. When I sit in my office working, they'll look through the glass door, throw up a heart, and get right back to playing. Overall, I can tell that this jump has been exhilarating for everyone's mind, body, and spirit.

I'm reminded of something I watched on Instagram that included that concept . . . of feeling exhilarated. In the video, during some sort of adult education class, a student raises their hand and asks why a dog sticks its head out the car window, even when bugs will certainly fly into its eyes. The instructor pauses and then replies, "It must be a small price to pay for the exhilaration of the ride." I loved that answer and decided to tell Hope about the dog theory during her nightly bath. The tub was filled with tons of suds from Mr. Bubble, and her little head was all that was showing. When she held her breath and sank down below the water, she popped back up to me warning her, "Hopey! You're going to get soap in your eyes!" She grinned and said, "Small price to pay . . ." Cute and clever, right?

In the days ahead, perhaps something exhilarating is out there waiting for you, pesky bugs and all. If you hear a whisper and it doesn't stop—to do something or try something or go somewhere—you should listen. Whispers tend to fade away if they're ignored long enough. I hope you allow yourself to visualize what change might look like for you. To imagine what the good stuff *and* the struggles would feel like. There's no harm in that; in fact, there's power. Realizing you're worth the effort is so very powerful.

My home office now includes a framed poem my friend Jane gave me. It's her way of turning my whisper into words on a page.

> *Feel the shift? It's underway.*
> *You're headed for a new today.*
> *The next awaits, wild and free.*
> *Time to climb another tree.*

The shift truly is underway, and this climb—as expected—has me finding my footing. And it's fun! I've been building Joy 101, learning as I go with a sensational but skeleton crew. Countless meetings and phone calls focus on everything from corporate sponsorships to health insurance. Every day, our vision takes shape, including an office renovation close to my house. (We found asbestos. Remember those inevitable bugs in the eyes?) I still call my mom every morning, but now I'm in my kitchen instead of on set at NBC. I can reach out to her during the day, too, which is new and wonderful. The ability to spend time with my family and friends whenever I want is pure freedom. No more, "I can only do it on the weekend and I have to be in bed early on Sunday." Flexibility adds so much meaning to my life, especially when it comes to my daughters' school activities. Can you volunteer for T-shirt making? Yes. Will you be there for Hope's 9 a.m. birthday party? Yes. From parent-teacher conferences to cupcake duty, I'm all in and it feels amazing.

I now use yellow legal pads to keep track of my daily schedule, and the stack is several inches high. There's lots of good stuff going on, and I'm endlessly grateful for this new chapter in my journey. Please hear my thank-you for the love and support you've always shown me and continue to do as I navigate "the next."

We'll be together again soon, but for now I'll leave you with one of my favorite quotes. It's a simple reminder for seekers—like you and me—who dare to awkwardly and excitedly and diligently search for ways to jump and find joy in this life. In this wild and precious life.

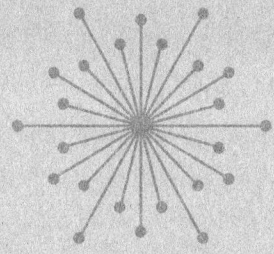

**"Tell me, what is it you plan to do with**

**your one wild and precious life?"**

—Mary Oliver

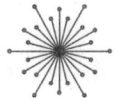

# Acknowledgments

IT'S NEVER LOST on me that I'm surrounded by exceptional people, and this book project reconfirmed how truly blessed I am.

Haley and Hope—My beautiful daughters, you are the "why" behind so many good decisions I make. Thanks for inspiring me to jump toward an exciting fresh start for us. You're my everything.

Maria Shriver—Thank you for pointing out my solid track record of embracing change. Until you ticked off the transitions I've made—from job to job, in personal relationships, into motherhood—I didn't feel brave enough to do something as scary as leaving NBC. I'm so grateful for your guidance, support, and for years of serving as my "what's possible." I love you, dear friend.

My NBC family—Without the solid springboard each of you helped me build year after year, I couldn't have launched to where I'm now headed. Thank you, and I can't wait to see you soon.

Richard Lovett—Most agents would have given me fifteen reasons *not* to leave NBC. But you just listened, as my friend. Then, when it was time to share the news with my bosses, you flew in and sat in the next room, just in case I needed anything. Wow. You're simply a remarkable person.

Cait Hoyt—One of the many things I love about you is that your ideas always focus on helping people. I think *Jump* will. Thank you for this book, your brilliance, and your caring heart.

The Putnam publishing team—Ivan Held, Ashley McClay, Alexis Welby, Lindsay Sagnette, Molly Pieper, Regina Andreoni, Katie Grinch, and Ashley Di Dio. This publishing stuff is easy, isn't it? HA! You all make it seem that way, and I can't thank you enough. I value your passion for creating meaningful work, and *Jump* certainly falls into that category because of you. A warm and special thank-you to executive editor Michelle Howry. Publishing always requires lots of bobbing and weaving, and you calmly and expertly led us through every hop, skip, leap, and jump. Thank you for making everyone feel heard, supported, and no matter the deadline, confident we'd beat the clock.

The Putnam production team—Maija Baldauf, Almudena Rincón, Katy Riegel, Erin Byrne, Janice Barral, Aja Pollock, Lorie Pagnozzi, Anthony Ramondo, and Monica Cordova. You folks are like butter—you make everything better. Once you polished the book inside and out, you grabbed the pom-poms and spread the word with grit and gusto. Thank you for your diligence, enthusiasm, and creativity. How fitting that the beautiful cover design practically JUMPS off the shelf!

Gina Sorell—You're a good human. Thank you for creating an effective and efficient road map we needed to navigate the

*Jump* journey. Because of your writing and organizing, we found our way.

Everyone featured in these pages—You are the nudge and North Star we need. Thank you for showing us your why and how.

Jane Lorenzini—You sit on Zooms with me for hours and hours, then place your fingers on the keyboard and hocus pocus . . . a beautiful book appears. At least that's how it looks to me. Janie, how do you keep getting better? I love you.

# About the Author

**Hoda Kotb** has claimed her role as one of America's foremost journalists, authors, and entertainers. Most well known as the former coanchor of NBC News' *Today* and cohost of *Today with Hoda & Jenna*, she is also the host of the popular podcast, *Making Space with Hoda Kotb*. Kotb joined *Today* as a cohost of the fourth hour in 2008, alongside Kathie Lee Gifford, and departed in 2024 following twenty-six successful years with the network. She is a *New York Times* bestselling author of the books *I Really Needed This Today*, *This Just Speaks to Me*, *Where We Belong*, *Hoda*, and *Ten Years Later*, as well as three children's books, *I've Loved You Since Forever*, *You Are My Happy*, and *Hope Is a Rainbow*. The four-time Emmy winner has also been honored multiple times with the Alliance for Women in Media's Gracie Award, as well as with the 2006 Peabody Award and the 2002 Edward R. Murrow Award. Hoda resides outside of New York City with her daughters, Haley and Hope.